*A COMMENTARY ON THE* VITA HADRIANI
*IN THE* HISTORIA AUGUSTA

*THE AMERICAN PHILOLOGICAL ASSOCIATION*
# AMERICAN CLASSICAL STUDIES

edited by
John Herington

NUMBER 7
*A COMMENTARY ON THE* VITA HADRIANI
*IN THE* HISTORIA AUGUSTA
Herbert W. Benario

*HERBERT W. BENARIO*

# A COMMENTARY ON THE *VITA HADRIANI* IN THE *HISTORIA AUGUSTA*

UNIVERSITY PRESS

Oxford University Press, Inc., publishes works that further Oxford University's objective of excellence in research, scholarship, and education.

Oxford  New York
Auckland  Cape Town  Dar es Salaam  Hong Kong  Karachi
Kuala Lumpur  Madrid  Melbourne  Mexico City  Nairobi
New Delhi  Shanghai  Taipei  Toronto

With offices in
Argentina  Austria  Brazil  Chile  Czech Republic  France  Greece
Guatemala  Hungary  Italy  Japan Poland  Portugal  Singapore
South Korea  Switzerland  Thailand  Turkey  Ukraine  Vietnam

Copyright © 1980 by The American Philological Association

Published by Oxford University Press, Inc.
198 Madison Avenue, New York, New York 10016
http://www.oup.com

Oxford is a registered trademark of Oxford University Press

All rights reserved.  No part of this publication may be reproduced, stored in a retrieval system, or transmitted, in any form or by any means, electronic, mechanical, photocopying, recording, or otherwise, without the prior permission of Oxford University Press.

Library of Congress Cataloging-in-Publication Data available

ISBN 978-0-89130-392-3

Printed in the United States of America
on acid-free paper

*Uxori carissimae hoc opus dedicat auctor: pro multo parvum*

## PREFACE

Well more than twenty years have passed since I first made serious acquaintance with the HA, and the present commentary was begun in the summer of 1975. Its progress limped along because of other academic obligations, but a Fellowship from the American Council of Learned Societies freed me from teaching during the winter and spring terms of 1978 and enabled me to spend eight months in close association with Hadrian. Part of that period I spent in Oxford, where I had access to the magnificant holdings of the Bodleian and Haverfield (Ashmolean) Libraries and where I was welcomed with great courtesy. I am grateful to ACLS and to the National Endowment for the Humanities which has bulwarked the Council's Fellowship program. When the manuscript was accepted for publication by the Editorial Board of the American Philological Association, I requested financial assistance from the administration of Emory University. Vice-President Charles T. Lester responded with alacrity and generosity; I thank both him and the University.

A first draft of part of the Commentary was read by Sir Ronald Syme, the entire work by Professor G.W. Bowersock and several anonymous referees. I have profited from the advice, criticism, and corrections of them all; they have saved me from various blunders and made the work richer and more penetrating. I have not always taken their advice; needless to say, responsibility for what follows rests with me alone.

The text that I have used is the standard edition of E. Hohl, *Scriptores Historiae Augustae* I (Leipzig: Teubner, 1927, reprint with addenda 1955). It is reproduced here by courteous permission of the publisher, B.S.B. Teubner Verlagsgesellschaft, Leipzig. The translations of Dio Cassius are those of E. Cary from the Loeb Classical Library edition (London: William Heinemann; New York: G.P. Putnam's Sons, 1925). That of Philostratus is by W.C. Wright in the Loeb Classical Library edition (London: William Heinemann; New York: G.P. Putnam's Sons, 1922).

The manuscript was first typed in final form by Mrs. Jill Goldsby. The camera ready copy was prepared by Mrs. June Mann. I am grateful to both for their skill and care.

References to modern scholars in the Commentary are by name alone, with addition of a numeral in parentheses where necessary; full information is given in the Bibliography. But E.M. Smallwood's invaluable *Documents Illustrating the Principates of Nerva,*

*Trajan and Hadrian*, to which reference is frequently made, is cited by name alone, followed by the number of the document.

                                             H.W.B.

Emory University
December 1979

TABLE OF CONTENTS

| | | |
|---|---|---|
| Introduction | | 1 |
| Text | | 15 |
| Commentary | | 43 |
| Appendix I | Hadrian's Family | 141 |
| Appendix II | Hadrian's career as *privatus* | 143 |
| Appendix III | Hadrian's Titulature | 145 |
| Appendix IV | The Chronology of Hadrian's Travels | 147 |
| Appendix V | Second and Third Consulates, Augustus through Hadrian | 151 |
| Appendix VI | Prosopographical Index | 153 |
| Bibliography | | 157 |

INTRODUCTION

The *Historia Augusta* is the title given to the collection of biographies of Roman emperors covering the years 117-284 (there is a gap for the years 244-260). Six different authors claim one or more of the lives apiece; many are dedicated either to Diocletian or to Constantine, with the consequence that a period of composition ending no later than 337 was long accepted.

Almost a century ago, Hermann Dessau first challenged the current beliefs on authorship and dates. He concluded that there was only one author, who wrote about the year 395. The intervening decades have seen an enormous amount of controversy, which has by no means subsided.

I shall not discuss the current status of HA studies. One of the great profits emanating from the emphasis placed upon the HA in the various publications of the participants in the Bonner Historia-Augusta-Colloquia has been a consensus that the collection of biographies is the work of one man at the very end of the fourth century A.D. Concomitant with that conclusion is the parallel one that the claim of the lives to be the product of six authors who dedicated their work to the Emperors Diocletian and Constantine is fraudulent. These are the views which I follow regarding authorship and date, and I shall, consequently, often speak of "our author" or "the author."

Coherent recapitulations of the trend of HA studies in the last quarter century and more, since the project of commentaries on the entire collection was first announced (see *Gnomon* 23 [1951] 293-4), can be found in the two surveys of A. Chastagnol, "Le Problème de l'Histoire Auguste: État de la question," *HAC Bonn 1963* (1964) 43-71, and "Les recherches sur l'Histoire Auguste de 1963 à 1969," *Recherches sur l'Histoire Auguste* (Bonn 1970) 1-37. Also immensely useful, and challenging, are the two volumes by Sir Ronald Syme, *Ammianus and the Historia Augusta* (Oxford 1968) and *Emperors and Biography. Studies in the Historia Augusta* (Oxford 1971).

Not all scholars, one must admit, have been won over to the views of single authorship late in the fourth century. Perhaps the most eloquent partisan of the traditional beliefs is A. Momigliano in a seminal paper, "An Unsolved Problem of Historical Forgery: The *Scriptores Historiae Augustae*," *Journal of the Warburg and Courtauld Institutes* 17 (1954) 22-46 = *Secondo*

*Contributo alla storia degli studi classici* (Rome 1960) 105-38, with two subsequent Appendices.

* * *

The standard for Latin biography from the second century A.D. on was Suetonius' *De Vita Caesarum*. A collection of twelve Lives from Julius to Domitian, it had enormous impact upon readers and self-styled continuators. Concerned with character above all, with judicious admixture of scandal and peculiarities of personality, the Lives entertained as they instructed, informing the reader of the main outlines of the subject's career and the type of person he was, while titillating his natural curiosity regarding the frailties of those who, in succession, were the *principes* of the Roman empire. Suetonius' sense of biography gave short shrift to other individuals and to the affairs of government, except as they directly impinged upon the subject. Such a presentation, neatly ordered in convenient sections, required less mental exertion than the broader sweep of history, particularly as practiced by a difficult writer such as Tacitus, and for this reason the biographical approach dominated Roman historical writing until late in the fourth century. Suetonius' contemporary, Plutarch, satisfied the demands of his Greek audience for moral presentations and comparisons of great figures in both Greek and Roman history.

Suetonius was little concerned with chronology; similar occurrences at different times are presented together, so that a pattern of behavior may be discerned. The result, in general, is that the reader sees a drama with only one major character, and that one in isolation. Nor is anything left to the reader's imagination; it is all spelled out. In the two fullest biographies, which are perhaps also the earliest, he sets out a programmatic statement, leading the reader by an intellectual hand:

> Talia agentem atque meditantem mors praevenit. de qua prius quam dicam, ea quae ad formam et habitum et cultum et mores, nec minus quae ad civilia et bellica eius studia pertineant, non alienum erit summatim exponere. (*Jul.* 44.4)

> Quoniam qualis in imperis ac magistratibus regendaque per terrarum orbem pace belloque re p. fuerit, exposui, referam nunc interiorem ac familiarem eius vitam quibusque moribus atque fortuna domi et inter suos egerit a iuventa usque ad supremum vitae diem. (*Aug.* 61.1)

# Introduction

Arrangement of material, in the denial of the importance of a chronological framework, is *per species* (*Aug.* 9). Categories dominate the structure of much of his work. And since the author of the HA has chosen to link his own work with Suetonius, among others, we shall have to ask how closely he has adhered to his model.

He claims credit for accuracy in presentation rather than for loftiness of style, and places himself squarely on the side of the biographers rather than of the historians:

> illud tantum contestatum volo me et rem scripsisse, quam, si quis voluerit, honestius eloquio celsiore demonstret, et mihi quidem id animi fuit, ut non Sallustios, Livios, Tacitos, Trogos atque omnes disertissimos imitarer viros in vita principum et temporibus disserendis, sed Marium Maximum, Suetonium Tranquillum, Fabium Marcellinum, Gargilium Martialem, Iulium Capitolinum, Aelium Lampridium ceterosque, qui haec et talia non tam diserte quam vere memoriae tradiderunt. (*Probus* 2.6-7)

That being the case, we are compelled to conclude that he has fallen far short of his model. He has nowhere given a programmatic statement in the *Vita Hadriani*, nor has he arranged his material *per species*, but he has rather produced a disjointed work, clearly drawn from several sources, which he has inelegantly and incompetently conflated. He thereby shows himself to be an artisan of ideas and words, stitching them together with insufficient regard for consistency and continuity of narrative, rather than a skilled master of his craft. And the whole bespeaks speed and carelessness: not a coherent literary effort but a compilation.

The structure of the *Vita Hadriani* falls easily into four large sections; further subdivision is, of course, possible, to make the analysis more acute.

1-4 Hadrian's family and early life up to his accession to the principate.

5.1-14.7 His life up to his final return to Rome, embracing historical events, general politics, his relations with the senate, his military reforms, his travels.

14.8-22 His character, legal concerns, civilian administration, building activities, games presented, literary tastes, acts of charity and kindness.

23-27 His life after his final return to Rome, the length of his life and reign, appearance, physical activities and pleasures, *signa mortis*, consecration and final character judgment.

At first glance it appears that the author's distribution of his material follows the Suetonian canon, but his mingling of historical details with character delineation, the blending of "narrative" and "description" (to recall Friedrich Leo's words *Erzählung* and *Beschreibung*), goes against that standard. The author may have wished to follow it, but his handling of his sources led to failure.

Even a cursory reading of the Life reveals a curious mingling of two traditions, one favorable to the emperor, the other quite the opposite. The former is sober and detailed, the latter anecdotal and miscellaneous. Unless we choose to give the author credit for greater independent research than seems suitable for his intellectual milieu, the obvious conclusion is that he is following two independent but parallel sources, which he has combined in such a way that there are numerous repetitions, many of them contradictory, doublets, and frequent dislocations of material, where items are introduced into the narrative in passages where they are obviously out of place. What were the sources that he used?

> I shall simply list them first, with comment to follow:
> The emperor's own autobiography;
> A biography by Marius Maximus;
> A biography by an unknown author;
> The series of biographies known as *Enmann's Kaisergeschichte*, which served as a common source for Aurelius Victor, Eutropius, and the *liber de Caesaribus* as well.

And we must allow him an occasional comment on his own account, revealing his own time and his use of his material.

Our author mentions Hadrian's autobiography five times, and in two other passages it is likely that this work is the source. But did the author pursue research in the emperor's own writing, or should we assign that task to the unknown author? Probably the latter, yet we cannot be sure. The autobiography was probably written upon Hadrian's return to Rome for the last time, so that it was a source through 14.5.

The major sources are the two biographies. To say two clearly indicates that I stand with those scholars, from Dürr to Syme and Barnes, who deny that Marius Maximus was the chief, and almost solitary, source. The debate continues, represented, e.g., by Syme's papers, "*Ignotus*, the Good Biographer," *HAC Bonn 1966/67* (1968) 131-52, and "Not Marius Maximus," *Hermes* 96 (1968) 494-502, and Barnes' book, *The Sources of the Historia Augusta* (Brussels 1978), for the anonymous author, and A.D.E.

Cameron, "Literary Allusions in the Historia Augusta," *Hermes* 92
(1964) 363-77, at 373, and A. Birley, *Septimius Severus* (London
1971) 308-26, for Marius Maximus. But I think that the general
consensus at present favors two biographers, one of whom we may,
with Syme, dub *Ignotus*.

Maximus wrote a series of twelve biographies, matching
his model Suetonius in number, covering the regnant *principes*
from Nerva to Elagabalus, excluding Verus. He was a senator,
with a magnificent career, for the details of which see the note
on 2.10. His work, as far as can be determined, focused upon
scandal and gossip, and the author of the HA reproaches him as
*homo omnium verbosissimus, qui et mythistoricis se voluminibus
inplicavit* (*Quad. Tyr.* 1.2). It seems hardly likely that such
a writer furnished the valuable material that abounds throughout
the Life. And it is odd that Marius Maximus' name is mentioned
only in connection with items which are unfavorable to Hadrian;
if he were the main source of the Life, whence come the sober
items that permeate the whole?

The key to the problem is the *Vita Veri*, which Barnes has
shown is a valuable contribution to the study of the second century; but we know that Maximus did not include a life of Verus
in his collection. When the author of the HA undertook to include, in addition to every emperor, everyone who was either
Caesar or pretender, he was compelled in most instances to call
upon his own imagination, except for Verus, for whom there already existed a sound biography.

There is a certain pattern of consistency and reliability
in the nine Lives from Hadrian to Caracalla, including that of
Verus; if we may postulate initial biographies of Nerva and
Trajan and then add Macrinus, we will realize a series of a
dozen for this unknown author as well. But that need not be;
*Ignotus* may have chosen to cease with Caracalla, the end, as it
seemed at the time, of the Severan dynasty, before the accession
to the purple of the first man of equestrian rank. For the
*Macrinus* begins with a preface unlike anything in the previous
Lives, strongly suggesting that the author's main prior source
has run out and he is now struggling with his own resources:
*Vitae illorum principum seu tyrannorum sive Caesarum, qui non
diu imperarunt, in obscuro latent, idcirco quod neque de privata
eorum vita digna sunt, quae dicantur, cum omnino ne scirentur
quidem, nisi adspirassent ad imperium, et de imperio, quod non
diu tenuerunt, non multa dici possunt: non tamen ex diversis*

*historicis eruta in lucem proferemus, et ea quidem quae memoratu digna erunt.*

*Ignotus*, then, to paraphrase Lécrivain, was the author of a biography which was straightforward, precise, trustworthy, favorable to Hadrian but on the whole impartial, which avoided generalizations, included only a few, brief anecdotes, and introduced no documents. The presentation was essentially chronological, with some attempt to order material *per species*.

The accretions, on the other hand, which have been largely drawn from Marius Maximus, are unfavorable to Hadrian and essentially biographical. He was concerned with personality, and wished to show the emperor as the enemy of the senate and as a man torn by personal failings and inner torments, a suitable pendant for the *optimus princeps*, Trajan, as, for Suetonius, Tiberius had been to Augustus.

The *Kaisergeschichte*, or KG, is a necessary assumption to explain the similarities among the epitomators of the fourth century. Conjectured by A. Enmann in 1884, its existence is now beyond dispute. The author of the HA may have used it directly, or may have drawn upon the epitomators.

Before we proceed to an analysis of the structure of the *Vita Hadriani*, let us record the references to the autobiography and to Marius Maximus, as well as other items which suggest these two sources.

From the autobiography:

1.1 *in libris vitae suae Hadrianus ipse commemoret*
3.3 *indulsisse vino se dicit*
3.4 *omen sibi factum adserit*
5.3 *ut dicebat*, reading the singular rather than *dicebant*
6.1-4 the correspondence with the senate
7.1 *cum etiam successorem Hadrianus sibimet destinasset*

In addition, there is reference to the autobiography in 16.1, *ut libros vitae suae scriptos a se libertis suis litteratis dederit iubens, ut eos suis nominibus publicarent.*

From Marius Maximus (stated):

2.10 *ut Marius Maximus dicit*
12.4 *ut verba ipsa ponit Marius Maximus*
20.3 *Marius Maximus dicit*
25.4 *quamvis Marius Maximus . . . commemoret*
16.7 *mathesin sic scire sibi visus est* = Ael. 3.9
*fuisse enim Hadrianum peritum matheseos Marius Maximus usque adeo demonstrat*

21.4  *inter cibos unice amavit tetrafarmacum* = *Ael.* 5.5
      *de quo genere cibi aliter refert Marius Maximus*

From Marius Maximus (inferred):

1.5   the name *Graeculus*
2.1   his passion for hunting
2.6-10 the scandal over his debt, his relations with
      the *paedagogi*, the prophecies, and Plotina's support
3.3   drinking with Trajan
4.1   Plotina's influence
4.5   the scandal over his relations with the *liberti* and
      *delicati*
4.8-10 Trajan's refusal to designate him as his successor
7.3   his *crudelitas*
9.1-3 his *crudelitas*
11.3-7 his *saevitia*
13.10 accusers of governors and procurators
14.1  his *odium* against Antioch
14.6  his responsibility for the death of Antinous
23.7  his *crudelitas*
23.10 Commodus' selection because of his *forma*
23.11 the words *invitis omnibus*
25.7  the words *invisus omnibus*

These instances, and more could undoubtedly be added, suggest the tenor of Maximus' narrative. The structure of the Life clearly displays the integration of material from Maximus and other sources, seldom identified, with the basic material offered by *Ignotus*.

The following chart suggests the sources of sections and phrases of the Life and how they have been conflated. Column A indicates the passages that go back to *Ignotus*, B those from Marius Maximus, and C those either from the KG or the author himself. This listing is, of course, highly speculative; other distributions are certainly possible.

| A | B | C |
|---|---|---|
| 1.1-5 | 1.5 *ingenio . . . diceretur* | |
| 2.1-3 | 2.4 | |
| 2.5 | 2.6-10 | |
| 3.1-3 | | 3.3 *ob hoc* (the author) |
| 3.4-5 | | 3.5 *unde hodieque* (the author) |

|        A              |        B                      |        C                              |
|-----------------------|-------------------------------|---------------------------------------|
| 3.6-4.1               | 4.1 *Plotinae favore*         |                                       |
| 4.1-3                 | 4.3 *inimicis suis*           |                                       |
| 4.4                   | 4.4 *favore Plotinae*         |                                       |
|                       | 4.5                           |                                       |
| 4.6-7                 | 4.8-10                        |                                       |
| 5.1-8.11              |                               | 6.3 *ut optimus* . . . *dignitatem* (the author) |
|                       | 9.1-5                         | 9.6 *summotis* . . . *imperium* (the author?) |
| 9.6 *Campaniam* - 11.2 |                              | 10.2 *hoc est* . . . *Traiani* (the author) |
|                       | 11.3-7                        | 11.3 *epistularum magistro* (the author) |
| 12.1-13.1             | 12.4 *ioculariter* . . . *Maximus* | 13.2 *ut ferunt* (the author or another source?) |
| 13.3-14.5             | 14.1 Antioch                  | 13.3 *ut dicitur* (the author)        |
|                       | 14.6-7          or            | 14.6 (KG)                             |
|                       | 14.8-16.7                     |                                       |
| 16.8-20.2             | 20.3 *Marius* . . . *eveniret* |                                      |
| 20.4-6                | 20.7-21.14                    |                                       |
| 22.1-14               | 23.1-9                        |                                       |
| 23.8 *quasi* . . . *imperii* |                         |                                       |
| 23.10-24.2            | 23.10 *forma commendatum*     |                                       |
|                       | 23.11 *invitis omnibus*   24.3-5 (KG) |                               |
| 24.6-11               | 24.12-25.4                    |                                       |
| 25.5-6                | 25.7-10                       |                                       |
| 25.11                 | 26.1-10                       |                                       |
| 27.1-3                |                               | 27.4 (the author)                     |

    Such a blending of material was bound to produce contradiction and repetition, if the author were not extremely careful and alert. As we have already indicated, those were not characteristics with which we can credit him, and, consequently, there are numerous passages where we find doublets, repetitions, or contradictions. The last constitute the largest category, and basically consist, as can be expected, of statements that are favorable and unfavorable to Hadrian on the same subject.

| Favorable/Accurate | Unfavorable/Inaccurate |
|---|---|
| 3.3 quando quidem et indulsisse vino se dicit Traiani moribus obsequentem atque ob hoc se a Traiano locupletissime muneratum. | 2.7 fuitque in amore Traiani, nec tamen ei per paedagogos puerorum, quos Traianus impensius diligebat, . . . |

Reasons for Trajan's favor

| | |
|---|---|
| 3.7 quare adamante gemma, quam Traianus a Nerva acceperat, donatus ad spem successionis erectus est. | 4.4-5 secundo consul favore Plotinae factus totam praesumptionem adoptionis emeruit. corrupisse eum Traiani libertos, curasse delicatos eosdemque saepe inisse per ea tempora, quibus in aula familiarior fuit, opinio multa firmavit. |

Reasons for hope of succession

| | |
|---|---|
| 4.6 legatus Suriae litteras adoptionis accepit | 4.8-10 Frequens sane opinio fuit Traiano id animi fuisse, ut Neratium Priscum, non Hadrianum successorem relinqueret, . . . |

Adoption by Trajan

| | |
|---|---|
| 5.3 quare omnia trans Eufraten ac Tigrim reliquit exemplo, ut dicebat Catonis, qui Macedonas liberos pronuntiavit, quia tueri non poterant. | 9.1-2 Inter haec tamen et multas provincias a Traiano adquisitas reliquit . . . . et haec quidem eo tristiora videbantur, quod omnia, quae displicere vidisset, Hadrianus mandata sibi ut faceret secreto a Traiano esse simulabat. |

Reasons for relinquishing the provinces

| | |
|---|---|
| 6.7 Marcium Turbonem post Mauretaniam praefecturae infulis ornatum Pannoniae Daciaeque ad tempus praefecit. | 7.3 Dacia Turboni credita, titulo Aegyptiacae praefecturae, quo plus auctoritatis haberet, ornato |

### Doublet

7.2 . . . in itinere senatu iubente, invito Hadriano, ut ipse in vita sua dicit, occisi sunt.

9.3 quia iam quattuor consularium occisorum, quorum quidem necem in Attiani consilia refundebat, premebatur invidia.

### The affair of the four consulars

7.3 ad conprimendam de se famam

7.3 ad refellendam tristissimam de se opinionem

### Doublet

7.3 Romam venit

5.10 Romam venit

### Doublet

8.7 ut, cum Attianum ex praefecto praetorii ornamentis consularibus praeditum faceret senatorem, nihil se amplius habere, quod in eum conferri posset, ostenderit.

9.3 cum Attiani, praefecti sui et quondam tutoris, potentiam ferre non posset, nisus est eum obtruncare, . . .

### Relations with Attianus

8.11 Serviano sororis viro, cui tantum detulit, ut ei venienti de cubiculo semper occurrerit, tertium consulatum . . . non petenti ac sine precatione concessit.

2.6 a Serviano, sororis viro (qui et sumptibus et aere alieno eius prodito Traiani odium in eum movit) diu detentus . . .

### Relations with Servianus

14.6 aliis eum devotum pro Hadriano asserentibus

14.6 aliis, quod et forma eius ostentat et nimia voluptas Hadriani.

### Reasons for Antinous' death

16.8 sed quamvis esset in reprehendendis musicis, tragicis, comicis, grammaticis, rhetoribus, oratoribus facilis, tamen omnes professores et honoravit

15.10 et quamvis esset oratione et versu promtissimus et in omnibus artibus peritissimus, tamen professores omnium artium semper ut doctior risit,

et divites fecit, licet eos        contempsit, obtrivit.
quaestionibus semper agitaverit.

   Relations with professors

16.10                              15.12-13
   Both sections, concluding discussion of Hadrian's literary abilities and his relations with various people, end with Favorinus.

17.1 Quos in privata vita          15.2 idem tamen facile de
inimicos habuit, imperator         amicis, quidquid insusurrabatur,
tantum neglexit, ita ut uni,       audivit atque ideo prope cunctos
quem capitalem habuerat, factus    vel amicissimos vel eos, quos
imperator diceret 'evasisti'.      summis honoribus evexit, postea
                                   ut hostium loco habuit

   Clemency to former enemies, cruelty to former friends

                                   15.8 Servianum sororis virum
                                   nonagesimum iam annum agentem,
                                   ne sibi superviveret, mori coegit
                                   23.2 de Serviano cogitavit,
                                   quem postea, ut diximus, mori
                                   coegit.
                                   23.8 senex nonagenarius . . .
                                   mori coegit
                                   25.8 Servianum nonaginta annos
                                   agentem, ut supra dictum est,
                                   ne sibi superviveret atque, ut
                                   putabat, imperaret, mori coegit

   Servianus put to death

17.5 omnes reges muneribus suis    17.10-11 regibus multis pluri-
vicit.                             mum detulit, a plerisque vero
                                   etiam pacem redemit, a nonnullis
                                   contemptus est, multis ingentia
                                   dedit munera,

   Generosity with gifts

17.9 frigora et tempestates ita    23.1 Peragratis sane omnibus
patienter tulit, ut numquam        orbis partibus capite nudo et
caput texerit.                     in summis plerumque imbribus

                                        atque frigoribus in morbum
                                        incidit lectualem.

   Doublet on his physical endurance

24.4-5 quamvis alii cognomen-   27.4 qua re, ut supra dictum
tum hoc ei dicant inditum, quod  est, multi putant Antoninum
multos senatores Hadriano iam   Pium dictum
saevienti abripuisset, alii,
quod ipsi Hadriano magnos
honores post mortem detulisset.

   Doublet on Antoninus' name of Pius

There is also a number of passages which have been inserted into the narrative in the wrong place, and thus break up the continuity of thought and development of a theme. Such passages are the following, which may be called dislocations:

7.1, with its talk of a successor to Hadrian, does not fit, for the context is the beginning of the reign. It would suit better in 23.

11.3-7 break up the narrative of Hadrian's presence in Britain (*Brittaniam petit* 11.2, *Conpositis in Brittania rebus* 12.1) by introducing personal material, with only the first part about Septicius Clarus and Suetonius belonging, on the assumption that their transgression and discharge occurred in Britain. The passage would fit well at the beginning of 15.

12.1 The uprising in Alexandria, stemming from the birth of a new Apis (itself unlikely), occurred in the first year of Hadrian's reign (Dio LXIX 8.1$^a$).

18.9 and 11 intrude in a narrative of Hadrian's actions to better the lot of slaves.

20.1-3, itemizing personality traits, interrupt the narrative of his building activity.

20.2 should have appeared after 14.4, during the course of his visit to Egypt.

20.6, mentioning the appointment of a *fisci advocatus*, belongs rather in the context of 7.6-7, where the problem of monies owing to the *fiscus* is mentioned.

20.7-21.4, containing personal items, intrude upon political and social notices.

22.12, the draining of the Fucine lake, belongs rather in the context of 19, where Hadrian's building activity is detailed.

22.14, the miracle of rain in Africa after a five year drought, fits more properly in 21.6, after a succession of natural occurrences.

23.5 speaks of Terentius Gentianus, who was dead long before this time. He should have been mentioned in 15.

25.8, with its repetitious report of Servianus' enforced suicide, interrupts the narrative of Hadrian's last days. The death occurred earlier than this period.

26.4-5, briefly mentioning some of Hadrian's literary and building tastes, tell little of his personality, and belong rather in the contexts of 16 and 19.

The *Vita Hadriani* does not offer a rounded biography of Hadrian. There are many gaps, which must be filled from other sources. But since Hadrian was such a complex individual, the ideal biography may never be written; certainly one does not presently exist. Nonetheless, the reader may wish to consult one or more of the following, which furnish discussions of the emperor and his career; they differ greatly, one from the other, not only in length and detail but in reliability.

- G. W. Bowersock, "Hadrian," *Encyclopedia Britannica* 8 ($1974^{15}$) 538-41
- A. Garzetti, *From Tiberius to the Antonines* (London 1974)
- S. Perowne, *Hadrian* (London 1960)
- E. T. Salmon, *A History of the Roman World from 30 B.C. to A.D. 138* (London $1968^6$) 295-318
- C. H. V. Sutherland and M. Hammond, "Hadrian," *OCD* ($1970^2$) 484-86
- R. Syme, *Tacitus* (Oxford 1958)

The fictional treatment by M. Yourcenar, *Hadrian's Memoirs* (New York 1954), is remarkably successful in evoking the character of the man.

Even though the *Vita Hadriani* is not a literary document of the first rank and is a poorly constructed exemplar of Latin biography, as the major literary source for the period it remains unique. Its importance for students of Rome will depend upon its historical integrity, which is quite high, as I hope the following commentary will reveal. There are many cases where independent confirmation exists from inscriptions, laws, coins, papyri, and archaeology; our author is far more frequently accurate than clearly wrong. Many of the errors are venial, few terribly misleading. All in all, one can read the *Vita* with considerable confidence.

The *Vita Hadriani*

## ⟨AELII⟩ SPARTIANI
# DE VITA HADRIANI

Origo imperatoris Hadriani vetustior a Picentibus, 1
posterior ab Hispaniensibus manat, si quidem Hadria
[h]ortos maiores suos apud Italicam Scipionum temporibus resedisse in libris vitae suae Hadrianus ipse commemoret. Hadriano pater Aelius Hadrianus cognomento 2
Afer fuit, consobrinus Traiani imperatoris, mater Domitia Paulina Gadibus orta, soror Paulina nupta Serviano, uxor Sabina, atavus Maryllinus, qui primus in
sua familia senator populi Romani fuit.

Natus est Romae VIIII. kl. Feb. Vespasiano septies 3 *a. r.*
et Tito quinquies consulibus. ac decimo aetatis anno 4 *n.76*
patre orbatus Ulpium Traianum praetorium tunc,
consobrinum suum, qui postea imperium tenuit, et
Caelium ⟨A⟩t[a]tianum equitem Romanum tutores habuit. imbutusque inpensius Graecis studiis, ingenio eius 5
sic ad ea declinante, ut a nonnullis Graeculus diceretur,
quinto decimo anno ad patriam redit ac statim militiam iniit, venando usque ad ⟨re⟩prehensionem studiosus. quare a Traiano abductus a patria et pro filio 2
habitus nec multo post decemvir litibus iudicandis da-

---

SPARTIANI DE VITA HADRIANI P (ad diocletianū aug̃. *add.
a. m.*) 5 hortos P¹ *ante ras.* italicam P¹ *t.* B itali∗am P
*corr.* 6/7 cõmemoret P¹ *t.* B cõmemorat P *corr.*, Σ 12 Romae] *sed Italica Hadriani patria esse videtur; cf Hieronym.
chron. 197 b) Helm* 14 tunc P¹ *t.* B uirum Σ, P *corr. in ras.*
16 tatianum P Attianum *Salm.; verum nomen est non* Caelius *sed* Acilius Attianus *(ILS 8999)* 20 uenandi *Nov.*
usque ad prẹhensionem P¹ *t.* B usq; ad reprẹhensionem P
*corr.*, Σ 21 troiano P¹ *t.* B 22 indicandis P¹ *t.* B

1∗

tus atque inde tribunus secundae Adiutricis legionis
3 creatus. post h⟨a⟩ec in inferiorem Moesiam transla-
4 tus extremis iam Domitiani[s] temporibus. ibi a mathematico quodam de futuro imperio id dicitur compe-
risse, quod a patruo magno Aelio Hadriano peritia cae-
5 lestium callente praedictum esse conpererat. Traiano a
Nerva adoptato ad gratulationem exercitus missus {in}
6 Germaniam superiorem translatus est. ex qua festinans
ad Traianum, ut primus nuntiaret excessum Nervae,
a Serviano, sororis viro, (qui et sumptibus et aere
alieno eius prodito Traiani odium in eum movit) diu
detentus fractoque consulte vehiculo tardatus, pedibus iter faciens eiusdem Serviani *beneficiar*⟨i⟩um ante-
7 venit. fuitque in amore Traiani, nec tamen ei per
p⟨a⟩edagogos puerorum, quos Traianus impensius di-
8 ligebat, † Gallo favente defuit. quo quidem tempore
cum sollicitus de imperatoris erga se iudicio Vergilianas sortes consuleret,

   'quis procul ille autem ramis insignis olivae
   sacra ferens? nosco crines incanaque menta
   regis Romani, primam qui legibus urbem
   funda*b*it, Curibus parvis et paupere terra
   missus in imperium magnum, cui deinde subibit',

sors excidit, quam alii ex S*i*byllinis versibus ei prove-
9 nisse dixerunt. habuit autem praesumptionem imperii
mox futuri ex fano quoque Niceforii Iovis manante
responso, quod Apollonius Syrus Platonicus libris suis
10 indidit. denique statim suffragante Sura ad amicitiam
Traiani pleniorem redit, nepte per sororem Traiani

---

2 hec P$\Sigma$ hoc *edd. cum* B   3 domitianis P$^1$ *t*. B -ani∗ P *corr.*
6 conpererat P$^1$ compererat P *corr.*   7 in *om.* P$^1$, *non om.* $\Sigma$,
*add.* P *corr.*   13 ueneficiarum *vel* -arium P$^1$ (-ar$\overset{i}{u}$ B) uene-
ficia∗∗∗ P *corr.* (beneficia *a. m. in marg.*) ueneficiarum R beneficiarium *Cas., edd.*   14 ei] et *Momms.*   16 Gallo] alio *Momms.;
post* Gallo *falso lacunam statuit Pet.; sed videtur aliquid inter-
cidisse*   17/18 uirgilianas $\Sigma$, P *corr.*   19 Aen. VI 808 *sqq.*
22 fundauit P, *em. Cas. ex* R   24 sybillinis P

uxore accepta favente Plotina, Traiano leviter, ut Marius Maximus dicit, volente.

Quaesturam gessit Traiano quater et Articuleio con- 3  *a. p. Chr.*
sulibus, in qua cum orationem imperatoris in senatu  *n. 101*
5 agrestius pronuntians risus esset, usque ad summam
peritiam et facundiam Latinis operam dedit. post 2
quaesturam acta senatus curavit atque ad bellum Dac⟨ic⟩um Traianum familiarius prosecutus est; quando 3
quidem et indulsisse vino se dicit Traiani moribus
10 obsequentem atque ob hoc se a Traiano locupletissime
muneratum. tribunus plebis factus est Candido et 4
Quadrato iterum conss., in quo magistratu ad perpe- 5  *a. p. Chr.*
tuam tribuniciam potestatem omen sibi factum adserit,  *n. 105*
quod p⟨a⟩enulas amiserit, quibus uti tribuni plebis
15 pluviae tempore solebant, imperatores autem numquam. unde hodieque imperatores sine paenulis a togatis videntur. secunda expeditione Dacica Traianus 6
eum primae legioni Minerviae praeposuit secumque
duxit; quando quidem multa egregia eius facta cla-
20 ruerunt. quare adamante gemma, quam Traianus a 7
Nerva acceperat, donatus ad spem successionis erectus
est. praetor factus est Sub[s]urano [bis] et Serviano 8
iterum conss., cum sestertium iterum vicies ad ludos
edendos a Traiano accepit. legatus postea pr⟨a⟩etorius 9
25 in Pannoniam inferiorem missus Sarmatas compressit,
disciplinam militarem tenuit, procuratores latius evagantes coercuit. ob hoc consul est factus. in quo ma- 10  *a. p. Chr. n. 108*

---

2 dicit P (it *a. m. in ras.*) 3 ar\*\*culeio P *corr.* (Σ) articuleio P¹ *t.* B      7 atq; P (t *in ras.*)      7/8 dacicum P¹ *t.* B dacum Σ, P *corr. per ras.* dacicum P *corr.*² *in ras.*      8 quanto P¹      22 subsurano bis P Suburano bis *Momms.* Suburano [bis] *He.; mendosa est utique consulatus notatio; nam Suranus est consul II a. p. Chr. n. 104 sed una cum altero collega; iterum consulatu functi sunt Sura et Servianus a. p. Chr. n. 102, quod non quadrat; praeturam iniit Hadrianus circa annum 106 (ILS 308)*      23 iterum *post* sestertium *del. Momms. (Jord.)*

gistratu *ut* a Sura conperit adoptandum se a Traiano
esse, ab amicis Traiani contempni desiit ac neglegi.
11 et def*un*cto quidem Sura Traiani ei familiaritas cre[a]-
vit, causa praecipue orationum quas pro imperatore[s]
4 dictaverat, usus Plotinae quoque favore, cuius studio
etiam legatus expeditionis Parthicae tempore destina-
2 tus est. qua quidem tempestate utebatur Hadrianus
amicitia Sosi Papi et Pl*a*tori Nepotis ex senatorio or-
dine, ex [s]equestri autem Attiani, tutoris quondam sui,
3 et Liviani ⟨*et*⟩ Turbonis. in adoptionis sponsionem
venit Palma et Celso, inimicis semper suis et quos
postea ipse insecutus est, in suspicionem ad*f*ec⟨*ta*⟩tae
*a. p.* 4 tyrannidis lapsis. secundo consul favore Plotinae fac-
*Chr.*
*n.118* 5 tus totam praesumptionem adoptionis emeruit. corrupisse eum Traiani libertos, curasse delicatos eosdem-
que s⟨*a*⟩epe i⟨*n*⟩isse per ea tempora, quibus in aula
6 familiarior fuit, opinio multa firmavit. quintum iduum August. die⟨*m*⟩ legatus Suriae litteras adoptionis
accepit, quando et natalem adoptionis celebrari iussit.
7 tertium iduum earundem, quando et natalem imperii
statuit celebrandum, excessus ei Traiani nuntiatus est.
8  Frequens sane opinio fuit Traiano id animi fuisse, ut
Neratium Priscum, non Hadrianum successorem relin-
queret, multis amicis in hoc consentientibus, usque eo
ut Prisco aliquando dixerit: 'commendo tibi provin-
9 cias, si quid mihi fatale contigerit.' et multi quidem
dicunt Traianum in animo id habuisse, ut exemplo

---

1 & P ut P *corr. in marg.*    3 definito P¹ *t.* B defūcto P
*corr.*    3/4 cre∗uit PB (a *eras.?*) crebuit *Pet.*    4 imperatores P¹ *t.* B -ore∗ P *corr.*    8 pl&ori P Σ Platori *Borghesi*
(*Pet.*)    9 sequestri P¹ *t.* B ∗equ- P *corr.*    10 et *add. Hirschf.*
(*cf. PIR II p. 339 nr. 179*)    11/12 quos postea P¹ *t.* B quō̊
postea P *corr.*    12 adiectę P adfectae *Salm., edd.* adfectatae *Petsch.* (*Less.*)    16 sepelisse P Σ saepe linxisse *Momms.*
saepe inisse *Ell., de Wi.*    17 familiariorum *Pet. cum* B    quintū
P¹ quinto Σ, P *corr.*    18 august' P    suriae P¹ *t.* B syriae P
*corr.*    20 tertiū P tertio Σ

Alexandri Macedonis sine certo successore moreretur,
multi ad senatum eum orationem voluisse mittere
⟨pe⟩titurum, ut, si quid ei evenisset, principem Ro-
manae rei publicae senatus daret, additis dum taxat
nominibus ex quibus optimum idem senatus eligeret.
nec desunt qui factione Plotinae mortuo iam Traiano
Hadrianum in adoptionem adscitum esse prodiderint,
supposito qui pro Traiano fessa voce loquebatur.

Adeptus imperium ad priscum se statim morem instituit et tenendae per orbem terrarum paci operam
intendit. nam deficientibus his nationibus, quas Traianus subegerat, Mauri lacessebant, Sarmat⟨a⟩e bellum
inferebant, Brittanni teneri sub Romana dicione non
poterant, Aegyptus seditionibus urgebatur, Libya denique ac Pal⟨a⟩estina rebelles animos efferebant. quare
omnia trans Eufraten ac Tigrim reliquit exemplo, ut
diceba[n]t Catonis, qui Macedonas liberos pronuntia-
vit, quia tueri non poterant. Part⟨h⟩amasirin, quem
Traianus Parthis regem fecerat, quod eum non magni
ponderis apud Parthos videret, proximis gentibus dedit
regem.

Tantum autem statim clementiae studium habuit, ut,
cum sub primis imperii diebus ab Attiano per episto-
las esset admonitus, ut et B⟨a⟩ebius Macer praefectus
urbis, si reniteretur eius imperio, necaretur et Laberius Maximus, qui suspectus imperio in insula exu-
labat, et Frugi Crassus, neminem laederet; quamvis
Crassum postea procurator egressum insula, quasi res
novas moliretur, iniusso eius occiderit. militibus ob

---

3 titurū P¹ iturum R iterum A    8 loquebatur P¹ *t*. B loque-
retur Σ, P *corr. in ras.*    11 intendit P¹ *t*. B (intendit *in marg.
adn. a. m. in* P) dedit Σ impendit P *corr.*    14 licya P litia Σ
Libya *Cas. (Pet.)*    15 afferebant PM efferebant Σ    17 dicebant P dicebat Σ    18 tueri] *passive haud raro ponitur a iuris consultis; cf. Heumann-Seckel, Handlexikon zu den Quellen
des röm. Rechts, s. v.* poterat *Bae.* sarmatosirin P Parthamo-
sirim *Cas.* Parthamasirin *Dess.; intellegendus est Parthamaspates,
cf. PIR III p. 13 nr. 98*    29 iniusso P iussu Σ

8 auspicia imperii duplicem largitionem dedit. Lusium
Quietum sublatis gentibus Mauris, quos regebat, quia
suspectus imperio fuerat, exarmavit Marcio Turbone
Iudaeis conpressis ad deprimendum tumultum Maure-
9 taniae destinato. post haec Antiochia[m] digressus est
ad inspiciendas reliquias Traiani, quas Attianus, Plo-
10 tina et Matidia deferebant. quibus exceptis et navi
Romam dimissis ipse Antiochiam regressus praepo-
sitoque Syriae Catilio Severo per Illyricum Romam
6 venit. Traiano divinos honores datis ad senatum et
quidem accuratissimis litteris postulavit et cunctis vo-
lentibus meruit, ita ut senatus multa, quae Hadrianus
non postulaverat, in honorem Traiani sponte decer-
2 neret. cum ad senatum scriberet, veniam petit, quod
de imperio suo iudicium senatui non dedisset, salu-
tatus scilicet praepropere a militibus imperator, quod
3 esse res publica sine imperatore non posset. cum
triumphum ei senatus, qui Traiano debitus erat, detulisset, recusavit ipse atque imaginem Traiani curru
triumphali vexit, ut optimus imperator ne post mor-
4 tem quidem triumphi amitteret dignitatem. patris patriae nomen delatum sibi statim et iterum postea
distulit, quod hoc nomen Augustus sero meruisset.
5 aurum coronarium Italiae remisit, in provinciis minuit,
et quidem difficultatibus aerarii ambitiose ac diligenter expositis.
6 Audito dein tumultu Sarmatarum et Roxalanorum
7 praemissis exercitibus Moesiam petit. Marcium Turbonem post Mauretaniam praefecturae infulis ornatum

---

1 duplicem *om.* P*ᵃ*, *add.* P*ᵇ*   2 gentilibus *Momms.* quos
P *Σ (Schmalz, Lat. Syntax § 34 et 46 cft. He.; v. c. 11, 5)* quas
*Kell. (Pet.)*   4 iudęi P*ᵃ* iudęis P*ᵇ*   4/5 mauritaniae P *in ras.*
*(corr. ex* mauretaniae *t.* B)   10 datis ad senatū P¹ *t.* B darī a senatu P *corr. in ras.*   17 rei publice P¹ res publica P *corr.*   27 regis
alanorum P *corr. in ras.* rex alanorum P¹ *t.* B Roxolanorum *Cas.*
Roxalanorum *Pet.*   29 maurataneae P¹ *t.* B mauritaniae P *corr.
in ras.* Mauretaniam *Pet. (c. 13, 6 post* Africam *cft. He.)* Maure-

Pannoniae Daciaeque ad tempus praefecit. cum rege 8
*R*oxalanorum, qui de imminutis stipendiis querebatur,
cognito negotio pacem conposuit.
　Nigrini insidias, quas ille sacrificanti Hadriano con- 7
scio sibi Lusio et multis aliis paraverat, cum etiam
successorem Hadrianus sibimet destinasset, evasit.
quare Palma Tarracenis, Celsus Bais, Nigrinus Fa- 2
ventiae, Lusius in itinere senatu iubente, invito Hadriano, ut ipse in vita sua dicit, occisi sunt. unde 3
statim Hadrianus ad refellendam tristissimam de se
opinionem, quod occidi passus esset uno tempore quattuor consulares, Romam venit Dacia Turbo*ni* credita,
titulo Aegyptiacae praefecturae, quo plus auctoritatis
haberet, ornato[s], et ad conprimendam de se famam
congiarium duplex praesens populo dedit ternis iam
per singulos aureis se absente divisis. in senatu quo- 4
que excusatis, quae facta erant, iuravit se numquam
senatorem nisi ex senatus sententia puniturum. sta- 5
t*um* cursum fiscalem instituit, ne magistratus hoc
[h]onere gravarentur. ad colligendam autem gratiam 6
nihil praetermittens infinitam pecuniam, quae fisco de-
bebatur, privatis debitoribus in urbe atque Italia, in
provinciis vero etiam ex reliqui[i]s ingentes summas
remisit syngrafis in foro divi *Tra*iani, quo magis securitas omnibus roboraretur, incensis. damnatorum 7
bona in fiscum privatum redigi vetuit omni summa
in aerario publico recepta. pueris ac puellis, quibus 8
etiam Traianus alimenta detulerat, incrementum libe-
ralitatis adiecit. senatoribus, qui non vitio suo de- 9
coxerant, patrimonium pro liberorum modo senatoriae
professionis explevit, ita ut plerisque in diem vitae

---

taniae ⟨administrationem⟩ *Momms.* Mauretaniae ⟨curam⟩ *Schenkl*
　2 mox alanorum P*Σ*　　12 turbone P¹　　14 ornatos P¹
ornatus *Σ*, P *corr.*　　18/19 stati̅ P*Σ* statum *Juret (Pet.)* (*cf.
Hirschf. V.-B.² p. 192, adn. 1*)　　20 honore P¹ onere *Σ*, P *corr.*
23 reliquiis P¹　　24 in *om.* Pᵃ, *add.* Pᵇ　　hadriani P (at traiani
*superscr. a. m.*) trayani *Σ*　　30 liberorum ⟨numero⟩ ? *He.*

10 suae dimensum sine dilatione ⟨p⟩r⟨a⟩estiterit. ad honores explendos non solum amicis, sed etiam passim
11 aliquantis multa largitus est. feminas nonnullas ad
12 sustentandam vitam sumptibus iuvit. gladiatorium
munus per sex dies continuos exhibuit et mille feras
8 natali suo edidit. optumos quosque de senatu in con-
2 tubernium imperatoriae maiestatis adscivit. ludos cir-
3 censes praeter natalicios decretos sibi sprevit. et in
contione et in senatu saepe dixit ita se rem publicam
gesturum, ut sciret populi rem esse, non propriam.
4 tertio consules, cum ipse ter fuisset, plurimos fecit,
infinitos autem secundi consulatus honore cumulavit.

*a. p. Chr. n. 119* 5 ipsum autem tertium consulatum et quattuor mensi-
6 bus tantum egit et in eo saepe ius dixit. senatui legitimo, cum in urbe vel iuxta urbem esset, semper inter-
7 fuit. senatus fastigium in tantum extulit difficile faciens senatores, ut, cum At*tia*num ex praefecto praetorii ornamentis consularibus praeditum faceret senatorem, nihil se amplius habere, quod in eum conferri
8 posset, ostenderit. equites Romanos nec sine se de
9 senatoribus nec secum iudicare permisit. erat enim
tunc mos, ut, cum princeps causas agnosceret, et senatores et equites Romanos in consilium vocaret et sen-
10 tentiam ex omnium deliberatione proferret. exsecratus est denique princ*ip*⟨e⟩s, qui minus senatoribus detu-
11 lissent. Serviano sororis viro, cui tantum detulit, ut
ei venienti de cubiculo semper occurrerit, tertium consulatum, nec secum tamen, cum ille bis ⟨ante⟩ Hadrianum fuisset, ne esset secundae sententiae, non petenti ac sine precatione concessit.
9 Inter haec tamen et multas provincias a Traiano

---

1 restiterit P¹ restituerit Σ, P *corr.* praestiterit *Cas., edd.*
1/2 hores Pᵃ honores Pᵇ  2 passim P a̅l̅ pessimis *superscr. a. m.*
pessimis Σ  6 Optumos P¹ Opti∗mos P *corr.* 10 scirent *Ell.*
11 c̄o̅s̅. P  17 atutinum P¹ attianum P *corr.* 25 princeps P¹
principes P *corr.* 26 cui *in* P *lineola transfixum* 28 ante
*om.* P¹Σ  29 non *in* P *a. m. in ras.*

adquisitas reli[n]quit et theatrum, quod ille in campo
Martio posuerat, contra omnium vota destruxit. et 2
haec quidem eo tristiora videbantur, quod omnia, quae
displicere[nt] vidisse⟨t⟩, Hadrianus mandata sibi ut
faceret secreto a Traiano esse simulabat. cum Attiani, 3
praefecti sui et quondam tutoris, potentiam ferre non
posset, nisus est eum obtruncare, sed revocatus est,
quia iam quattuor consularium occisorum, quorum
quidem necem in Attiani consilia refundebat, premebatur invidia. cui cum successorem dare non posset, 4
quia non petebat, id egit, ut peteret, atque, ubi primum petit, in Turbonem transtulit potestatem; cum 5
quidem etiam Simili alteri praefecto Septicium Clarum successorem dedit. summotis his a praefectura[e], 6
quibus debebat imperium, Campaniam petit eiusque
omnia oppida beneficiis et largitionibus sublevavit
optimum quemque amicitiis suis iungens. Romae vero 7
praetor[i]um et consulum officia frequentavit, conviviis amicorum interfuit, aegros bis ac ter die, et nonnullos equites Romanos ac libertinos, visitavit, solaciis
refovit, consiliis sublevavit, conviviis suis semper ad-
hibuit. omnia denique ad privati hominis modum fecit. 8
socrui suae honores praecipuos inpendit ludis gladia- 9
toriis ceterisque officiis.
    Post haec profectus in Gallias omnes c⟨ivit⟩a⟨te⟩s 10
variis liberalitatibus sublevavit. inde in Germaniam 2
transiit pacisque magis quam belli cupidus militem,
quasi bellum inmineret, exercuit tolerantiae documen-
tis eum imbuens, ipse quoque inter manipula vitam
militarem magistrans, cibis etiam castrensibus in pro-

---

1 relinquit P¹   2 marcio P   4 displicerent uidisse P¹ t. B¹
displicere ** uidisset P corr., Σ   5 decr&o PΣ secreto Momms.
(edd.)   7 nisus P¹ x superscr. a. m.   9/10 pręmebatur P
11 putebat P¹ t. B   18 pr&orium P¹   19/20 et nonnullos
equites Romanos ac libertinos post subleuauit transposuit Uhl.
    25 casuarlis PΣ causarios Egn. (Pet.) eas uarils Momms. ciui-
tates uarils Rös., Damsté   27 transit Pᵃ transiit Pᵇ t. B   29 eum]
eos Σ uel eos superscr. a. m. in P   30 catrensibus Pᵃ, corr. Pᵇ

patulo libenter utens, hoc est larido, caseo et posca,
exemplo Scipionis Aemiliani et Metelli et auctoris sui
Traiani, multos praemiis, nonnullos honoribus donans,
3 ut ferre possent ea, quae asperius iubebat; si quidem
ipse post C⟨a⟩esarem Octavianum labantem disciplinam incuria superiorum principum retinuit ordinatis
et officiis et inpendiis, numquam passus aliquem a
castris iniuste abesse, cum tribunos non favor militum,
4 sed iustitia commendaret, exemplo etiam virtutis suae
ceteros adhortat*us*, cum etiam vicena milia pedibus
armatus ambularet, triclinia de castris et porticus et
5 cryptas et topia dirueret, vestem humillimam frequenter acciperet, sine auro balteum sumeret, sine gem-
mis fibula ⟨*sagum*⟩ stringeret[ur], capulo vix eburneo
6 spatham clauderet, aegros milites in hospi*t*iis suis
videret, locum castris caperet, nulli vitem nisi robusto
et bonae famae daret nec tribunum nisi plena barba
faceret aut eius aetatis, quae prudentia et annis tri-
7 bunatus robor inpleret, nec pateretur quicquam tribunum a milite accipere, delicata omnia undique summo-
veret, arma postremo eorum supe*l*lectilemque corri-
8 geret. de militum etiam aetatibus iudicabat, ne quis
aut minor quam virtus posceret, aut maior quam pateretur humanitas, in castris contra morem veterem
versaretur, agebatque, ut sibi semper noti esse⟨*nt*⟩, et
11 eorum numerus sciretur. laborabat praeterea, ut con-
di[c]ta militaria diligenter agnosceret, reditus quoque
provinciales solerter explorans, ut ⟨*si*⟩ alicubi quip-
piam deesset, expleret. ante omnes tamen enitebatur,
ne qui*d* otiosum vel emeret aliquando vel pasceret.

---

5 octauianū P¹ *t*. B octaui∗∗ū P *corr.*     7/8 ac∗astris P
(r *eras.*)     10 adhortatos P¹ *t*. B     14 sagum *add. Ho.*
stringer&ur PΣ stringeret *Pet.*     15 hospiciis P     16 uitem]
aurem Σ a*t* utrem *superscr. a. m. in* P     19 robor P¹ *t*. B
robur P *corr.*     21 superlectilemq: P¹ *t*. B suppellectilemq: P
*corr.*     25/26 esse et eorum P¹ *t*. B essent & eorum P *corr.*
*in ras.*, Σ     26/27 condicta PΣ     28 ut P¹ ne Σ ut si P *corr.*
30 nequit P¹ *t*. B nequid P *corr.*

Ergo conversis regio more militibus Brittaniam petit, 2
in qua multa correxit murumque per octoginta milia
passuum primus duxit, qui barbaros Romanosque divideret.
Septicio Claro praefecto praetorii et Suetonio Tran- 3
quillo epistularum magistro multisque aliis, quo*d* apud
Sabinam uxorem *in* [i]us[s]u eius familiarius se tunc
egerant, quam reverentia domus aulicae postulabat, successores dedit, uxorem etiam ut morosam et asperam
dimissurus, ut ipse dicebat, si privatus fuisset. et erat 4
curiosus non solum domus suae sed etiam amicorum,
ita ut per frumentarios oc⟨c⟩ulta omnia exploraret,
nec adverterent amici sciri ab imperatore suam vitam, priusquam ipse hoc imperator ostenderet. unde 5
non iniocundum est rem inserere, ex quo constet eum
de amicis multa didicisse. nam cum ad quendam 6
scripsisset uxor sua, quod voluptatibus detentus et lavacris ad se redire nollet, atque hoc Hadrianus per
frumentarios cognovisset, petente illo commeatum Hadrianus ei lavacra et voluptates exprobravit. cui ille:
'num et tibi uxor mea, quod et mihi, scripsit?' et hoc 7
quidem vitiosissimum putant atque huic adiungunt,
quae de adultorum amore ac nuptarum adulteriis, quibus Hadrianus laborasse dicitur, adserunt, iungentes
quod ne amicis quidem servaverit fidem.
Conpositis in Brittania rebus transgressus in Gal- 12
liam Alexandrina seditione turbatus, quae nata est ob
Apidem, qui, cum repertus esset post multos annos,
turbas inter populos creavit, apud quem deberet locari, omnibus studiose certantibus. per idem tempus 2
in honorem Plotinae basilicam apud Nemausum opere
mirabili extruxit. post haec Hispanias petit et Tarra- 3

---

3 qui] ut et Σ ut *superscr. a. m. in* P  6 quos PΣ quod *Gru., edd.*  7 uniussu eius P¹ iniussu eius P *corr.* in usu eius *Petsch. (Pet.)*  9 murosam P¹ *t.* B morosam Σ, P *corr.*  15 quo PΣ (*cf. c. 5, 8* gentibus — quos) qua *edd.*  23 adultorū P¹ *t.* B adultorū (*i. e.* adulterorum) P *corr.* adulterorum Σ

cone hiemavit, ubi sumptu suo *ae*dem Augusti resti-
4 tuit. omnibus Hispanis Tarraconem in conventum vocatis dilectumque ioculariter, ut verba ipsa ponit Marius Maximus, retractantibus Italicis, vehementissime
5 ceteris prudenter caute⟨*que*⟩ consuluit. quo quidem
tempore non sine gloria gravissimum periculum adiit
apud Terraconem spatians per virdiaria servo in se
hospitis cum gladio furiosius inruente[m], quem reten-
tum ille ministris adcurrentibus tradidit et, ubi furio-
sum esse constitit, medicis curandum dedit in nullo
6 omnino commotus. per ea tempora et alias frequenter
in p*l*urimis locis, in quibus barbari non fluminibus
sed limitibus dividuntur, stipitibus magnis i*n* modum
muralis saepis funditus iactis atque conexis barbaros
7 separavit. Germanis regem constituit, motus Maurorum compressit et a senatu supplicationes emeruit.
8 bellum Parthorum per idem tempus in motu tantum
13 fuit, idque Hadriani conloquio repressum est. post
haec per Asiam et insulas ad Achaiam navigavit et
Eleusinia sacra exemplo Herculis Philippique suscepit,
multa in Athenienses contulit et pro agonotheta rese-
2 dit. et in Achaia quidem etiam illud observatum ferunt,
quod, cum in sacris multi cultros haberent, cum Ha-
3 driano nullus armatus ingressus est. post in Siciliam
navigavit, in qua Aetnam montem conscendit, ut solis
4 ortum videret arcus specie, ut dicitur, varium. inde
Romam venit atque ex ea in Af⟨*r*⟩icam transiit ac
multum beneficiorum provinciis Africanis adtribuit.
5 ne⟨*c*⟩ quisquam fere principum tantum terrarum ta[n-
6 tu]m celeriter peragravit. denique cum post Africam

---

1 eadem P    2 tarraconā P¹ *t*. B tarraconē P *corr.*    5 caute P
et caute Σ cauteque *Bra. propter clausulam; asyndeton def.
Ti. p. 46*    7 uirdiaria P¹ uiridiaria P *corr.*    8 inruentē P¹
*t.* B, *virgulam erasit* P *corr.*    12 prurimis P¹ *t.* B    13 sti-
pib; Pᵃ, *corr.* Pᵇ  im modū P    14 muralis PΣ ruralis *Ohl.*
26 uarium] *def. Sjögren* uarum *vel* curuum *Hirschf.*    27 afi-
cā P¹    29/30 tantum celeriter P R

Romam redisset, statim ad orientem profectus per Athenas iter fecit atque opera, quae apud Athenienses coeperat, dedicavit, ut Iovis Olympii aedem et aram sibi, eodemque modo per Asiam iter faciens templa sui nominis consecravit. deinde a Capadocibus servitia castris profutura suscepit. toparchas et reges ad amicitiam invitavit, invitato etiam Osdroe rege Parthorum remissaque illi filia, quam Traianus ceperat, ac promissa sella, quae itidem capta fuerat. cumque ad eum quidam reges venissent, ita cum his egit, ut eos p⟨a⟩eniteret, qui venire noluerunt, causa speciatim Farasmanis, qui eius invitationem superbe neglexerit. et circumiens quidem provincias procuratores et praesides pro factis supplicio adfecit, ita severe ut accusatores per se crederetur inmittere. Antiochenses inter haec ita odio habuit, ut Syriam a Phoenice separare voluerit, ne tot civitatum metropolis Antiochia diceretur. moverunt ea tempestate et Iudaei bellum, quod vetabantur mutilare genitalia. sed in monte Casio, cum videndi solis ortus gratia nocte ascendisset, imbre orto fulmen[e] decidens hostiam et victimar⟨i⟩um sacrificanti adflavit. peragrata Arabia Pelusium venit et Pompei tumulum magnificentius extruxit. Antinoum suum, dum per Nilum navigat, perdidit, quem muliebriter flevit. de quo varia fama est aliis eum devotum pro Hadriano adserentibus, aliis, quod et forma eius ostentat et nimia voluptas Hadriani. et Graeci quidem volente Hadriano eum consecraverunt oracula per eum dari adserentes, quae Hadrianus ipse conposuisse iactatur.

Fuit enim poematum et litterarum nimium studio-

---

3 eadem P¹   6 Toparchas PM (tetra *superscr. a. m. in* P) toparcas A tetrarcas R   7 osdroe P¹ cosdroe P *corr.*   10 quidem P quidam Σ   14 pęsides Pᵃ, *corr.* Pᵇ   21 fulmine P¹ *t.* B fulmineo Σ fulmen∗ P *corr.* dicidens P¹ decidens P *corr.*   21/22 uictimarum P¹ uictimas P *corr.* uictimarium A   30 conposuisse P¹ composuisse P *corr.*

9 sissimus. arithmeticae, geometriae, picturae peritissimus. iam psallendi et cantandi scientiam prae se ferebat. in voluptatibus nimius. nam et de suis dilectis multa versibus composuit. [amatoria carmina scrip-
10 sit.] idem armorum peritissimus et rei militaris scien-
11 tissimus, gladiatoria quoque arma tractavit. idem severus laetus, comis gravis, lascivus cunctator, tenax liberalis, simulator ⟨dissimulator⟩, saevus clemens et semper in omnibus varius.
15 Amicos ditavit et quidem non petentes, cum petenti-
2 bus ni[hi]l negaret. idem tamen facile de amicis, quidquid insusurrabatur, audivit atque ideo prope cunctos vel amicissimos vel eos, quos summis honoribus evexit, postea ut hostium loco habuit, ut Attianum et Ne-
3 potem et Septicium Clarum. nam Eud⟨a⟩emonem prius
4 conscium imperii ad egestatem perduxit, Pol⟨y⟩aenum
5 et Marcellum ad mortem voluntariam coegit, Helio-
6 dorum famosissimis litteris lacessivit, Titianum ut conscium tyrannidis et argui passus est et proscribi.
7 Umidium Quadratum et Cat*i*lium Severum et Tur-
8 bonem graviter insecutus est, Servianum sororis virum nonagesimum iam annum agentem, ne sibi supervi-
9 veret, mori coegit; libertos denique et nonnullos mi-
10 lites insecutus est. et quamvis esset oratione et versu promtissimus et in omnibus artibus peritissimus, tamen professores omnium artium semper ut doctior
11 risit, contempsit, obtrivit. cum his ipsis professoribus et philosophis libris vel carminibus invicem editis saepe
12 certavit. et Favorinus quidem, cum verbum eius quondam ab ⟨H⟩adriano reprehensum esset atque ille ces-

---

4 5 amatoria carmina scripsit *glossema esse videtur omnibus codicibus inculcatum; del. Cas., edd.*   8 dissimulator *add. Ho. (cf. Sallust. Catil. 5, 4:* simulator ac dissimulator; *Epit. de Caes. 14, 6 de Hadriano:* simulans ... dissimulans*)*   11 nil *de Wi. propter clausulam*   16 Polęnū P Polyaenum *vulg. (Jord.)*
20 catalium PΣ   29/30 eius quondam P eius quoddam Σ quoddam eius *Sed. Scott. in exc., quod probat Momms.*

sisset, arguentibus amicis, quod male cederet Hadriano
de verbo, quod idonei auctores usurpassent, risum
iocundissimum movit; ait enim: 'non recte suadetis, 13
familiares, qui non patimini me illum doctiorem omnibus credere, qui habet triginta legiones.'
    Famae celebris Hadrianus tam cupidus fuit, ut li- 16
bros vitae suae scriptos a se libertis suis litteratis
dederit iubens, ut eos suis nominibus publicarent; nam
et Phlegontis libri Hadriani esse dicuntur. catacannas 2
libros obscurissimos Antimachum imitando scripsit.
Floro poetae scribenti ad se: 3

        ego nolo C⟨a⟩esar esse,
        ambulare per Brittanos,
        ⟨latitare per .........,⟩
        Scythicas pati ⟨p⟩ruinas
rescripsit: 4

        ego nolo Florus esse
        ambulare per tabernas,
        latitare per popinas,
        culices pati rutundos.

amavit praeterea genus vetustum dicendi. controver- 5
sias declamavit. Ciceroni Catonem, Vergilio En⟨n⟩ium, 6
Salustio Coelium praetulit eademque iactatione de Homero ac Platone iudicavit. mathesin sic scire sibi visus 7
est, ut sero kalendis Ianuariis scripserit, quid ei toto
anno posset evenire, ita ut eo anno, quo perit, usque
ad illam horam, qua est mortuus, scripserit, quid ac-

---

1 leder& P¹ *t.* B¹ ceder& P *corr.*, Σ    7 litteris Pᵃ litteratis
Pᵇ    9 catacannas P¹ *t.* B, M catacaimos P *corr.* catacaymos Σ
catachannas *Bernh.; cf. Thes. l. L. III, 586 (de nomine proprio
liberti Hadriani hariolatur Gerth, P.-W. X, 2450)*    14 latitare
per ... *add.* Gemoll *(Pet.)* latitare per Germanos *Rös.*    15 ru-
inas P¹Σ    *post* pruinas *omisso tertio versu* gladios pati cruen-
tos *suppl. Birt*    20 culices P¹ calices Σ, P *corr.* rutundos P¹
rotundos Σ, P *corr.*    21 amabit P¹    22 uergilio P¹ uirgilio P
*corr.*    enium P¹ *t.* B    25 sero] semper *Momms.* fere *? He.
an* sero kalendas Ianuarias *(pro* sero pridie kal. Ian.*) ? Ho.*

8 turus esset. sed quamvis esset in reprehendendis musicis, tragicis, comicis, grammaticis, r⟨h⟩et[h]oribus, oratoribus facilis, tamen omnes professores et honoravit et divites fecit, licet eos quaestionibus semper agi-
9 taverit. et cum ipse auctor esset, ut multi ab eo tristes recederent, dicebat se graviter ferre, si quem tristem
10 videret. in summa familiaritate Epictetum et ⟨H⟩eliodorum philosophos et, ne nominatim de omnibus dicam, grammaticos, r⟨h⟩et[h]ores, musicos, geometras, pictores, astrologos habuit, prae ceteris, ut multi ad-
11 serunt, eminente Favorino. doctores, qui professioni suae inhabiles videbantur, ditatos honoratosque a professione dimisit.
17 Quos in privata vita inimicos habuit, imperator tantum neglexit, ita ut uni, quem capitalem habuerat, fac-
2 tus imperator diceret 'evasisti'. his, quos ad militiam ipse per se vocavit, equos, mulos, vestes, sumptus et
3 omnem ornatum semper exhibuit. saturnalicia et sigillaricia frequenter amicis inopinantibus misit et ipse
4 ab his libenter accepit et alia invicem dedit. ad deprehendendas obsonatorum fraudes, cum plurimis simmatibus pasceret, fercula de aliis mensis etiam ultimis
5 quibusque {iussit sibi} adponi. omnes reges muneribus suis vicit. publice frequenter et cum omnibus la-
6 vit. ex quo ille iocus balnearis innotuit: nam cum quodam tempore veteranum quendam notum sibi in militia dorsum et ceteram partem corporis vidisset adterere ⟨parieti⟩, percontatus, cur se marmoribus destringendum daret, ubi audivit hoc idcirco fieri, quod servum non haberet, et servis eum donavit et sumptibus.
7 verum alia die cum plures senes ad provocandam libe-

---

4 eo P<sup>a</sup> eos P<sup>b</sup>   7 miliaritate P<sup>a</sup> familiaritate P<sup>b</sup>   10 astrologas P¹ *t*. B   11 faborino P¹   21/22 sūmatib; P summantibus Σ sigmatibus *Bernh. (Jord.)* simmatibus *Pet.*   23 quiq; P<sup>a</sup> quib;q; P<sup>b</sup>   adponi P¹ iussit adponi P *corr.* iussit sibi adponi (apponi) Σ adponit *Pet.*   28 parieti *add. Kell. (Pet.)*

ralitatem principis parieti[s] se adtererent, evocari eos
iussit et alium ab alio invicem defricari. fuit et plebis 8
iactantissimus amator. peregrinationis ita cupidus, ut
omnia, quae legerat de locis orbis terrarum, praesens
5 vellet addiscere. frigora et tempestates ita patienter 9
tulit, ut numquam caput texerit. regibus multis pluri- 10
mum detulit, a plerisque vero etiam pacem redemit,
a nonnullis contemptus est, multis ingentia dedit mu- 11
nera, sed nulli maiora quam Hiberorum, cui et ele-
10 phantum et quinquagenariam cohortem post magnifica
dedit dona. cum a F⟨a⟩rasmane ipse quoque ingentia 12
munia dona accepisset atque inter haec auratas quoque clamydes, trecentos noxios cum auratis clamy[mi]-
dibus in harenam misit ad eius munera deridenda.
15   Cum iudicaret, in consilio habuit non amicos suos 18
aut comites solum sed iuris consultos et praecipue
Iu⟨ven⟩tium Celsum, Salvium Iulianum, Neratium Priscum aliosque, quos tamen senatus omnis probasset.
constituit inter cetera, ut in nulla civitate domus ali- 2
20 qua[e] transferend⟨a⟩e ad aliam urbem vilis mate-
riae causa dirueretur. liberis proscriptorum duodeci- 3
mas bonorum concessit. maiestatis crimina non admi- 4
sit. ignotorum heredidates repudiavit nec notorum 5
accepit, si filios haberent. de thesauris ita cavit, ut, 6
25 {si} quis in suo rep⟨p⟩erisset, ipse potiretur, si quis
in alieno, dimidium domino daret, si quis in publico,
cum fisco aequabiliter partiretur. servos a dominis 7

---

  1 parietis P¹ t. B¹ parieti P corr. in ras.   3 iactantissim' P
accuratissimus Σ at accuratissimus in P superscr. a. m.   6 te-
xer& P¹ t. B texerit Σ, edd. teger& P corr., Sed. Scott. in exc.
  9 qui PΣ   11 dono Cas. (Pet.) dona del. Momms. (Jord.)
Petsch. dona def. Ti. p. 32   13/14 clamymidib; P¹ t. B¹ (mi
exp. P corr.)   15 consilia P   17 iuliū PΣ Iuuentium Cas.,
edd. (cf. PIR II p. 186 et p. 255 nr. 590)   neraciū P   19/20 ali-
quę P   20 ullis P¹ ulli' * (i. e. ullius) P corr. ulla Σ uilis
Momms. utilis Cornelissen   21 diruer&ur P¹ diruer&ur P corr.
  25 si om. P¹ t. B, non om. Σ   26 dimidiū domidiū domino P ͣ domidiū del. P t. B

2*

occidi vetuit eosque iussit damnari per iudices, si digni
essent. lenoni et lanistae servum vel ancillam vendi
vetuit causa non praestita. decoctores bonorum suorum, si su⟨a⟩e auctoritatis essent, catomidiari in
amphitheatro et dimitti iussit. ergastula servorum et
liberorum tulit. lavacra pro sexibus separavit. si dominus in domo interemptus esset, non de omnibus
servis quaestionem haberi sed de his, qui per vicinitatem poterant sentire, praecepit.

**19** In Etruria praeturam *im*perator egit. per Latina oppida dictator et aedilis et duumvir fuit, apud Neapolim
demarc⟨h⟩us, in patria sua quinquennalis et item Hadriae quinquennalis, quasi in alia patria, et Athenis
arc⟨h⟩on fuit.

In omnibus paene urbibus et aliquid aedificavit et
lu*d*os edidit. Athenis mille ferarum venationem in
stadio exhibuit. ab urbe Roma numquam ullum venatorem aut scaenicum avocavit. Romae post ceteras
inmensissimas voluptates in honorem socrus suae aromatica populo donavit, in honorem Traiani balsama
et crocum per gradus theatri fluere iussit. fabulas
omnis generis more antiquo in theatro dedit, histriones
aulicos publicavit. in circo multas feras et saepe centu⟨m⟩ leones interfecit. militares pyrric⟨h⟩as populo
frequenter exhibuit. gladiatores frequenter spectavit.
cum opera ubique infinita fecisset, numquam ipse nisi
in Traiani patris templo nomen suum scripsit. Romae instauravit Pantheum, s⟨a⟩epta, basilicam Neptuni, sacras ⟨a⟩edes plurimas, forum Augusti, lavaccrum Agrippae, eaque omnia propriis *a*uctorum no-

---

2 lęnoni P   lonistae Pᵃ, *corr.* Pᵇ   6 libertorum Σ   ₊tulit *pro* sustulit *propter clausulam ?* He.   10 inperator P   16 lusos P¹ lusus P *corr.*¹ ludos P *corr.*²   18 uocault Pᵃ auocauit Pᵇ aduocauit Σ   20 horem Pᵃ, *corr.* Pᵇ   23/24 conto P¹M centū P *corr.* (*cf. Cass. Dion. LXIX 8, 2 ...* λέοντας ἑκατὸν *κτλ.*) cunctos Σ   28 pantheum P¹A pantheon R, P *corr.*   30 agrippę P¹ agrippine Σ, P *corr.*   auctorum *Pet. coll. Suet.*

minibus consecravit. fecit et sui nominis pontem et 11
sepulchrum iuxta Tiberim et aedem Bonae Deae. trans- 12
tulit et colossum stantem atque suspensum per De-
crianum architectum de eo loco, in quo nunc templum
Urbis est, ingenti molir·ine, ita ut operi etiam elephan-
tos viginti quattuor exhiberet. et cum hoc simulacrum 13
post Neronis vultum, cui antea dicatum fuerat, Soli
consecrasset, aliud tale Apollodoro architecto auctore
facere Lunae molitus est.
 In conloquiis etiam humillimorum civilissimus fuit, 20
detestans eos, qui sibi han⟨c⟩ voluptatem humanitatis
quasi servantes fastigium principis inviderent. apud 2
Alexandriam in musio multas quaestiones professoribus proposuit et propositas ipse dissolvit. Marius 3
Maximus dicit eum natura crudelem fuisse et idcirco
multa pie fecisse, quod timeret, ne sibi idem, quod
Domitiano accidit, eveniret. et cum titulos in operibus 4
non amaret, multas civitates Hadrianopolis appellavit,
ut ipsam Karthaginem et ⟨At⟩henarum partem. aqua- 5
rum ductus etiam infinitos hoc nomine nuncupavit.
fisci advocatum primus instituit. fuit memoriae ingen- 6.7
tis, facultatis inmensae; nam ipse orationes et dictavit et ad omnia respondit. ioca eius plurima exstant; 8
nam fuit etiam dicaculus. unde illud quoque innotuit,
quod, cum cuidam canescenti quiddam negasset, eidem
iterum petenti sed infecto capite respondit 'iam hoc
patri tuo negavi'. nomina plurimis sine nomenclatore 9
reddidit, quae semel et congesta simul audiverat, ut
nomenclatores saepius errantes emendarit. dixit et 10

---

*Domit. 5* & ueterū P *quod def. Ti. p. 137; sed in Pantheo etiam-
nunc exstat auctoris Agrippae neque restitutoris Hadriani titu-
lus (ILS 129) et ueteribus* Σ   11 han P¹   12 seruantis P
seruantes *Roos*   13 im musio P   14 dissoruit Pᵃ, *corr.* Pᵇ
19 Karthaginē & henarū P¹   22 orationes & P *quod def. Ti.
p. 113 et orationes edd.* orationes et ⟨epistulas⟩ *He.*   23 ioca]
in P. *corr. ex* loca   24 sqq. *cf. Auson. epigr. de Myrone qui
Laidis noctem rogaverat. XXXVIII [XVII] p. 326 ed. Peiper*
29 emendauit PΣ

veteranorum nomina, quos aliquando dimiserat. libros
statim lectos et ignotos quidem plurimis memoriter
11 reddidit. uno tempore scripsit, dictavit, audivit et cum
amicis fabulatus est [si potes⟨t⟩ credi]. omnes publicas
rationes ita complexus est, ut domum privatam quivis
12 paterfamilias diligens non satis nov⟨er⟩it. equos et
13 canes sic amavit, ut eis sepulchra constitueret. op⟨p⟩i-
dum Hadrianotheras in quodam loco, quod illic et
feliciter esset venatus et ursam occidisset aliquando,
constituit.
21 De iudici[bu]s omnibus semper cuncta scrutando
2 tamdiu requisivit, quamdiu verum inveniret. libertos
suos nec sciri voluit in publico nec aliquid apud se
posse, dicto suo omnibus superioribus principibus vi-
tia imputans libertorum, damnatis omnibus libertis
3 suis, quicumque se de eo iactaverant. unde extat etiam
illud seueru⟨m⟩ quidem sed prope ioculare de servis.
nam cum quodam tempore servum suum inter duos
senatores e conspectu ambulare vidisset, misit, qui ei
collafum daret ⟨diceret⟩que: 'noli inter eos ambulare,
4 quorum esse adhuc potes servus.' inter cibos unice
amavit tetrafarmacum, quod erat de fasiano, sumine,
perna et crustulo.
5 Fuerunt eius temporibus fames, pestilentia, terrae
motus, quae omnia, quantum potuit, procuravit mul-
6 tisque civitatibus vastatis per ista subvenit. fuit etiam

---

2 statim] strictim *Pet.*     4 *post* fabulatus (confabulatus *Σ*)
est *add.* P *in contextu* si potes (potest P *corr.*) credi; *glossema
om.* *Σ*     6 non satis nouit P*Σ*; *del. Haupt* non setius norit
*Momms. (Pet.)* non satis nouerit (*scil.* prae imperatoris rei publicae scientia) *Ho.*     11 iudicib; P indicibus ?*Cas.* iudicis (*pro*
iudiciis) *He.*     14 dicto suo] *cf. AS 65, 5*     17 seuero P[1] se-
uere *Σ*, P *corr.* seuerum *Petsch.* saeue *Bernh. (Pet.) (cf. Norden,
Germ. Urgesch. in Tac. Germ. p. 51, adn. 5)*     20 colla funda-
ret qui noli P[1] *t.* B colaphum daretque noli Ch R colaphum
daret dicens noli A colafum daret et diceret noli P *corr. (a. m.
in ras.)*     22 amabit P[1] amabat P *corr.*     tętrafarmacum P
fasiono P[1]

Tiberis inundatio. Latium multis civitatibus dedit, tri- 7
buta multis remisit.
   Expeditiones sub eo graves nullae fuerunt; bella 8
etiam silentio p⟨a⟩ene transacta. a militibus propter 9
curam exercitus nimia*m* multum amatus est, simul
quod in eos liberalissimus fuit. Parthos in amicitia 10
semper habuit, quod inde regem retraxit, quem Traianus inposuerat. Armeniis regem habere permisit, cum 11
sub Traiano legatum habuissent. ⟨a⟩ Mesopoten*is* 12
non exegit tributum, quod Traianus inposuit. Alba- 13
nos et Hiberos amicissimos habuit, quod reges eorum
largitionibus prosecutus est, cum ad illum venire contempsissent. reges Bactranorum legatos ad eum ami- 14
citiae petend⟨a⟩e causa supplices miserunt.
   Tutores saepissime dedit. disciplinam civilem non 22
aliter tenuit qu*a*m militarem. senatores et equites Ro- 2
manos semper in publico togatos esse iussit, nisi si
a cena reverterentur. ipse, cum in Italia esset, semper 3
togatus processit. ad convivium venientes senatores 4
stans excepit semperque aut pallio tectus discubuit aut
toga summissa. diligentia iudic*is* sumptus convivii con- 5
stituit et ad anticum modum redegit. vehicula cum 6
ingentibus sarcinis urbem ingredi prohibuit. sederi
equos in civitatibus non sivit. ante octavam horam 7
in publico neminem nisi aegrum lavari passus est.
ab epistolis et a libellis primus equites Romanos ha- 8
buit. eos, quos pauperes et innocentes vidit, sponte 9
ditavit, quos vero calliditate ditatos, etiam odio habuit. sacra Romana diligentissime curavit, peregrina 10
contempsit. pontific*is* maximi officium peregit. causas 11
Romae atque in provinciis frequenter audivit adhibitis
in consilio suo consulibus atque praetoribus et op-

---

5 nimiae P¹ *t.* B nimiā∗ P *corr.*    9 a *add. Less.*    Meso-
potamenos P¹ *t.* B Mesopotamiis ∗∗ P *corr. in ras.*    18 cę-
na P    21 iudices P iudicis *Salm., edd.*    22 anticū P (q *a. m.*)
30 pontifices P¹

**12.13** timis senatoribus. Fucinum lacum emisit. quattuor con-
**14** sulares per omnem Italiam iudices constituit. quando in Africam venit, ad adventum eius post quinquennium pluit, atque ideo ab Africanis dilectus est.

**23** Peragratis sane omnibus orbis partibus capite nudo et in summis plerumque imbribus atque frigoribus in
**2** morbum incidit lectualem. factusque de successore sollicitus primum de Serviano cogitavit, quem postea, ut
**3** diximus, mori coegit. Fuscum, quod imperium praesagiis et ostentis agitatus speraret, in summa detestatione
**4** habuit. Platorium Nepotem, quem tantopere ante dilexit, ut veniens ad eum aegrotantem Hadrianus in-
**5** pune non a⟨d⟩mitteretur, suspicionibus adductus, e[s]t eodem modo et Terentium Gentianum, et hunc vehe-
**6** mentius, quod a senatu diligi tunc videbat, omnes postremo, de quorum imperio cogitavit, quasi futu-
**7** ro⟨s⟩ imperatores detestatus est. et omnem quidem vim crudelitatis ingenit⟨a⟩e usque eo repressit, donec in villa Tiburtina profluvio sanguinis p⟨a⟩ene ad ex-
**8** itum venit. tunc libere Servianum quasi affectatorem imperii, quod servis regi⟨i⟩s [s]c[a]enam misisset, quod in sedili regio iuxta lectum posito sedisset, quod erectus ad stationes militum senex nonagenarius proces⟨s⟩isset, mori coegit multis aliis interfectis vel
**9** aperte vel per insidias. quando quidem etiam Sabina uxor non sine fabula veneni dati ab Hadriano defuncta est.
**10** Tunc Ceionium Commodum, Nigrini generum insidiatoris quondam, sibi forma commendatum adoptare
**11** constituit. adoptavit ergo Ceionium Commodum Ve-

---

7 lectualem P¹ letalem P *corr.* (c *et* u *exp.*), Σ    8/9 *c. 15, 8*
11 pletoriū P Platorium *Borghesi (Pet.)*    12/13 inpune non amitter&ur P non impune admitteretur Σ    13 adductus ē. P adductus; et *Jord.*    16/17 futuro P¹Σ    18 ingenuae Pᵃ ingeni**te Pᵇ *t.* B    20 libere] liuore *Momms.*    21 scęnam P scenam (sceuam A) Σ strenam *Sca.*    23/24 procesiss& P
25 aparte Pᵃ, *corr.* Pᵇ

rum invitis omnibus eumque A⟨e⟩lium Verum Caesarem appellavit. ob cuius adoptationem ludos circen- 12
ses dedit et donativum populo ac militibus expendit.
quem pr⟨a⟩etura honoravit ac statim Pannoniis in- 13
posuit decreto consulatu[s] cum sumptibus. eundem $^{a.p.Chr.}_{n.137}$
Commodum secundum consulem designavit. quem cum 14
minus sanum videret, saepissime dictitavit: 'in caducum
parietem nos inclinavimus et perdidimus quater milies
sestertium, quod populo et militibus pro adoptione
Commodi dedimus.' Commodus autem prae valetudine 15
nec gratias quidem in senatu agere potuit Hadriano de
adoptione. denique accepto largius antidoto ingra- 16
vescente valetudine per somnum perit ipsis kalendis
Ianuariis. quare ab Hadriano Votorum causa lugeri
est vetitus. et mortuo [h]Aelio Vero Caesare Hadria- 24
nus ingruente tristissima valetudine adoptavit Arrium
Antoninum, qui postea Pius dictus est, et ea ⟨qui⟩dem
lege, ut ille sibi duos adoptaret, Annium Verum et
Marcum Antoninum. hi sunt qui postea duo pariter 2
Augusti primi rem publicam gubernaverunt. et An- 3
toninus quidem Pius idcirco appellatus dicitur, quod
socerum fessum aetate manu sublevaret. quamvis alii 4
cognomentu⟨m⟩ hoc ei dicant inditum, quod multos
senatores Hadriano iam saevienti abripuisset, alii, quod 5
ipsi Hadriano magnos honores post mortem detulisset.
Antonini adoptionem plurimi tunc factam esse dolue- 6
runt, speciatim ⟨C⟩atilius Severus, praefectus urbi, qui

---

1 aliū P¹ aeliū P *corr.*   2 adoptionem Σ, *edd.*   5 consulatus cum sumptib; P senatus consulto Σ (ł. s. c. *superscr. a. m. in* P)   15 & mortuo P, *quod def. Ti. p. 63 sed* mortuo *Cas. ex* R   hęlio P   17 & eadem PΣ et ea quidem *Jord.* (*Pet.²*)
18/19 Annium Verum et Marcum Antoninum] *confusa sunt nomina; Antoninus Pius adoptavit M. Annium Verum i. e. Imp. Caes. M. Aurelium Antoninum Augustum et L. Ceionium Commodum i. e. Imp. Caes. L. Aurelium Verum Augustum*   23 cognomento P   24 abripuiss& P subripuisset Σ   24/25 alii — detulisset] *om.* Pᵃ, *add.* Pᵇ *in marg. inf.*

7 sibi praeparabat imperium. qua re prodita successore accepto dignitate privatus est.
8 Hadrianus autem ultimo vitae taedio iam adfectus
9 gladio se transfigi a servo iussit. quod cum esset proditum et in Antonini usque notitiam venisset, ingressis ad se praefectis et filio rogantibusque, ut ⟨a⟩equo animo necessitatem morbi ferret, iratus illis auctorem proditionis iussit occidi, qui tamen ab Antonino ser-
10 vatus est. statimque testamentum scripsit nec tamen actus rei publicae pr⟨a⟩etermisit, dicente Antonino parricidam se futurum, si Hadrianum adoptatus ipse pa-
11 teretur occidi. et post testamentum quidem iterum se est conatus occidere; subtracto pugione saevior factus est.
12 petit et venenum a medico, qui se ipse, ne
25 daret, occidit. ea tempestate supervenit quaedam mulier, quae diceret somnio se monitam, ut insinuaret Hadriano, ne se occideret, quod esset bene valiturus. quod cum non fecisset, esse[t] caecatam. iussam tamen iterum Hadriano eadem dicere atque genua eius osculare
2 ⟨oculos⟩ receptura⟨m⟩, si id fecisset. quod cum ex somnio implesset, oculos recepit, cum a⟨qua⟩, quae
3 in fano erat, ex quo venerat, oculos abluisset. venit et de Pannonia quidam vetus caecus ad febrientem Ha-
4 drianum eumque conti[n]git. quo facto et ipse oculos recepit, et Hadrianum febris reliquit. quamvis Marius Maximus haec per simulationem facta commemoret.
5 Post haec Hadrianus Baias petit Antonino Romae
6 ad imperandum relicto. ubi cum nihil proficeret, arcessito Antonino in conspectu eius apud ipsas Baias
7 perit die VI. iduum Iuliarum. invisusque omnibus se-

---

7 post ferret *Pet. transponendo inseruit* dicente Antonino — pateretur occidi *(v. 10 sqq.)*     13 est *del. Pet.*     18 e& (*i. e.* esset) P¹     19 eus Pᵃ, *corr.* Pᵇ     20 oculos *add. Da. post* receptura *in P a. m. add. in marg.* uisū     21 insomnio P ex somnio Σ insomnium *edd.*     21/22 aquę in fano P¹ aqua quę in fano P *corr.*, Σ     24 contingit P¹ t. B contiṇgit (n *exp.*) P *corr.* contigit Σ     30 VI∗iduū P¹     VI∗iduū P *corr.*

pultus est in villa Ciceroniana Puteolis. sub ipso mortis 8
tempore et Servianum nonaginta annos agentem, {ut}
supra dictum est, ne sibi superviveret atque, ut puta-
bat, imperaret, mori coegit et ob leves offensas plu-
5 rimos iussit occidi, quos Antoninus reservavit. et mo- 9
riens quidem hos versus fecisse dicit⟨ur⟩:
      animula vagula blandula
      hospes comesque corporis,
      quae nunc abibis in loca
10     pallidula rigida nudula
      nec ut soles dabis iocos!
tales autem nec multo[s] meliores fecit et Graecos. 10
  Vixit annis LX[X]II, mensibus V, diebus XVII. im- 11
peravit annis XXI, mensibus XI.
15   Statura fuit procerus, forma comptus, flexo ad pecti- 26
nem capillo, promissa barba, ut vulnera, qu⟨a⟩e in
facie naturalia erant, tegeret, habitudine robusta. equi- 2
tavit ambulavitque plurimum armisque et pilo se
semper exercuit. venatus frequentissime leonem manu 3
20 sua occidit. venando autem iugulum et costam fregit.
venationem semper cum amicis participavit. in con- 4
vivio tragoedias, comoedias, Attellanas, sambucas, lec-
tores, poetas pro re semper exhibuit. Tiburtinam villam 5
mire exaedificavit, ita ut in ea et provinciarum et lo-
25 corum celeberrima nomina inscriberet, velut Lycium,
Academian, Prytanium, Canopum, P⟨o⟩ecilen, Tempe
vocaret. et, ut nihil praetermitteret, etiam inferos finxit.
  Signa mortis haec habuit: natali suo ultimo, cum 6
Antoninum commendaret, praetexta sponte delapsa ca-
30 put ei *a*peruit. anulus, in quo imago ipsius sculpta 7
erat, sponte de digito delapsus est. ante diem natalis 8

---

  2 ut *om.* P, *non om.* Σ    2/3 *c. 15, 8; 23, 2; 8*    3 supraulue-
r& P superuiueret Σ *(cf. H 15, 8)*    6 dicit P¹    9 quae P
quo Σ *(an* quos — locos *? Ho.)*    20 costam P cossam A coxam
R    26 academian P¹ -am P *corr.* piciien P Poeciien *Egn.*
30 operuit PΣ

eius nescio qui ad senatum ululans venit; contra quem
Hadrianus ita motus est, quasi de sua morte loquere-
tur, cum eius verba nullus agnosceret. idem cum vellet
in senatu dicere[t] 'post filii mei mortem', 'post meam'
dixit. somniavit praeterea se a patre potionem sopori-
feram impetrasse. item somniavit a leone se oppres-
sum esse.

**27** In mortuum eum a multis multa sunt dicta. acta eius
inrita fieri senatus volebat. nec appellatus es⟨se⟩t
divus, nisi Antoninus rogasset. templum denique ei
pro sepulchro aput Puteolos constituit et quinquennale
certamen et flamines et sodales et multa alia, quae ad
honorem quasi numinis pertinerent. qua re, ut supra
dictum est, multi putant Antoninum Pium dictum.

---

1 qui* P    4 dicer& P¹ dicere* P *corr.*    9 est P$\Sigma$ esset
*edd.*    13/14 *c.* 24, 5    14 *post* putant *add.* ob hec $\Sigma$ *(superscr.*
P *corr.)* VITA DIVI HADRIANI EXPLICIT P

COMMENTARY

1.1 *origo . . . posterior*  The two adjectives indicate the difference between *origo* and *patria*. Hadrian's ancestors originally came from the town of Hadria in Picenum and were settled in Italica at the end of the Second Punic War; this new colony became the *patria* of the Spanish branch of the Aelii. We may assume that other Aelii continued to live in Hadria; for them *origo* and *patria* were identical. But one need not be born in one's *patria*; the parents could well be abroad for a great variety of reasons. Hadrian belonged to the *tribus Sergia* (see App. II), which was the tribe of Italica. The tribe would not be affected by birth either in Italica or elsewhere.

1.1 *in libris vitae suae*  Nothing survives of this autobiography. Peter, *HRR* II 117-18, gives half a dozen references to it, one of them this passage. Yet our author states (16.1) that Hadrian ordered freedmen to publish his autobiographical books under their own names: *nam et Phlegontis libri Hadriani esse dicuntur*.

1.2 *Hadriano pater*  For Hadrian's family connections in detail, showing his relationship with the Ulpii Traiani, see the stemma in App. I. Maryllinus (Marullinus) was not his *atavus* in the literal meaning of the word, for that would push him back several generations too far; the word *avus* would have been sufficient. No details of his senatorial career are known. The *cognomentum* of Hadrian's father, *Afer*, cannot be explained; he had reached the praetorship by the time of his death in 85/86. His cousin, M. Ulpius Traianus, the future emperor, gained the consulate in 91; he too might have become a consular had he lived. Hadrian's mother bears a good Italian name; her *patria*, Gades, the modern Cadiz, was a city which had long been Punic but whose Roman history matched that of Italica, from which it was some sixty miles distant. It was one of the wealthiest cities in the empire during the first century, reputed to have more men of equestrian census than any city in the empire other than Rome and Patavium. Servianus was a good match for Hadrian's sister, perhaps already a consular at the time of the marriage.

1.2 *uxor Sabina*  Trajan's sister Marciana, who died in 112, was mother of Matidia, whose daughter, Vibia Sabina, now became Hadrian's wife. The marriage was never a happy one, nor blessed with any offspring. But it was important in linking Hadrian even closer to the emperor; he was now related both by blood and by marriage. See 2.10, 11.3, 23.9

1.2 *atavus Maryllinus* Nothing more is known about him. He is perhaps fictional, with the intent of giving Hadrian more ancient senatorial ancestry.

1.3 *Romae* Hadrian's actual birthplace is a subject of dispute. Eutropius (VIII 6.1) says *Natus et ipse Italicae in Hispania*. Since Hadrian's tribe coincides with that of Italica, the epitomator may just have assumed that he was born in Spain. But the HA may well be right, since Rome is the less obvious of the choices. See 1.1 and Syme (5) 142-3. The year of birth is 76.

1.4 *decimo anno* In his tenth year or at the age of ten? The former would mean most of the year 85, the latter most of the year 86. Probably we should think of the earlier date.

1.4 *praetorium* M. Ulpius Traianus was born on September 18, 53, and was thus slightly more than twenty years older than Hadrian. Having performed his vigintivirate duties around 70, he accompanied his father to Syria, probably in 72, as *tribunus militum*, and served in the same capacity along the Rhine and Euphrates. He became *quaestor* c. 78 and *praetor* c. 84. It was subsequent to this that he became Hadrian's *tutor*.

1.4 *consobrinum* The meaning of the word here is different from that in 1.2. There it literally meant cousin; here it is used in a much more general sense of relationship. Hadrian was grandnephew to Trajan, as Octavius had been to Julius Caesar.

1.4 *Caelium Attianum* His full name, here wrongly presented, was P. Acilius Attianus. Two points are of importance in his relations with Hadrian: he was a πολίτης , hence from Italica (Dio LXIX 1.2) and he was praetorian prefect at Trajan's death, with a role to play in Hadrian's succession. As a fellow-townsman, he was an obvious choice as a *tutor*. See 15.2

1.5 *Graecis studiis* The mature Hadrian was a most devoted Philhellene. When his affection for things Greek began we do not know; it may indeed have been the case that his education in Rome lit the spark, or perhaps the author has tried to explain the predilections of the man by invoking early training. In all likelihood it was the former. Since the days of Nero, education had become increasingly Hellenic; the tide could not be stemmed by the Flavians. Indeed, Vespasian appointed a professor of Greek rhetoric along with Quintilian, who held the Latin chair. Hadrian's enthusiasm and keen intellect enabled him to move as an equal among the intelligentsia of the empire.

The use of the adverb *impensius* suggests disapproval; cf. Tacitus' judgment of Agricola's philosophical proclivities (*Agr.* 4.3): *se prima in iuventa studium philosophiae acrius, ultra quam concessum Romano ac senatori, hausisse, ni prudentia matris incensum ac flagrantem animum coercuisset.* The *tutores* must have thought that Hadrian's zeal was unsuitable for a young man who had a senatorial career before him, and so he was sent to the less corrupting atmosphere of Italica. There Latin would be dominant without competition from Greek, and *provincialis parsimonia* would also obtain. Juvenal speaks with bitterness of the *Graeculi*.

That Hadrian's Latin in his younger days was not all it should have been is clear from 3.1, where he is an object of derision because of his uneducated pronunciation, *agrestius pronuntians*. Since instruction in Greek preceded formal instruction in Latin, his overenthusiastic attention to the former must have produced an ever-increasing gap between his fluency and elegance in the one and the other. Residence in Spain focused attention on Latin, but would not help in eliminating elements of *rusticitas*; one thinks of Asinius Pollio's gibe at Livy's *Patavinitas*, which, whatever the full meaning of the word may be, must have included criticism of his manner of speech. See, in general, Bonner 97-111, Clarke 14-15, and Marrou 255-64.

2.1 *quinto decimo* In his fifteenth year or at the age of fifteen? See 1.4

2.1 *redit* The use of this verb does not give the lie to the claim that Hadrian was born in Rome, nor need one assume that he had made an earlier visit to Italica which is nowhere mentioned. We may interpret the verb to mean no more than that he went to the old country, the country of his ancestors, just as first-generation Americans often use the verb "return" when they speak of visiting the country of their parents.

2.1 *militiam* What this military service could be is difficult
to imagine, if it does not just refer to Hadrian's joining the
local *collegium iuvenum*, wherein he learned the rudiments of
military training. Such *collegia* frequently had headquarters
of their own, if one may extrapolate from the existence of a
*schola iuvenum* in Pompeii on the Via dell'Abbondanza. See
Bengtson 298 and 304.

2.1 *venando* Hadrian's enthusiasm for hunting is best underscored by noting his naming of a new city *Hadrianotherae* (20.13)
because he had had a good hunt there. There is general agreement now that the medallions above the side passageways of the
Arch of Constantine in Rome, depicting alternately scenes of
hunting and sacrifice, are taken from a Hadrianic monument.
See Lugli 314 and Nash 104ff. See also 26.3

2.2 *decemvir litibus iudicandis* When will this have been? He
went to Italica in the year 90, in all probability (see 1.5),
stayed there for an unspecified time, was recalled to Rome by
Trajan, now a consular, and soon afterward, *nec multo post*,
entered upon his first office, one of the vigintivirate. This
would perhaps have been in 93 or 94, soon after he had donned
the *toga virilis*; sixteen or seventeen were customary ages for
this ceremony.

  The biographer fails to mention two other posts within
the vigintivirate stage that Hadrian held: he was *praefectus
feriarum Latinarum* and *sevir turmae equitum Romanorum* (see
App. II). To be a *decemvir stlitibus iudicandis* in the
principate was a source of distinction, although the court of
the *centumviri* had taken over much of the earlier jurisdiction
of the court of ten. The post was a favored one in the vigintivirate, for, along with the *IIIviri monetales*, its holders
normally became *candidati imperatoris* for higher office. Tenure
of these two posts marked a young man out for advancement in
the emperor's service. See E. Birley (1). The sevirate was
not particularly unusual, but the prefecture was, when the
*Feriae Latinae* were being held. Trajan's influence must have
been paramount for his young relative and protege.

2.2 *tribunus* Hadrian was *tribunus militum* of three legions in
succession, a range of experience unparalleled in any other
career save that of L. Minicius Natalis, *consul* 139 (Smallwood
225). Hadrian's first legion was *II Adiutrix Pia Fidelis*,
the second *V Macedonica*, the third *XXII Primigenia Pia Fidelis*.

The years in which his service with each of these began were 95, 96, and 97. What were the provinces? The biographer informs us indirectly: the second was Lower Moesia, the third Upper Germany, of which Trajan was then governor. Controversy exists about the first; Pannonia is commonly suggested (Weber, Henderson, Perowne, among others), but Syme (5) 143 proposes Upper Moesia, focusing upon the position of the adjective in *post haec in inferiorem Moesiam translatus*. Trajan was adopted by Nerva late in the year 97; the season must already have been unfavorable when Hadrian rode from Lower Moesia, at the extreme eastern portion of the Danube, to Moguntiacum (Mainz) along the Rhine, where Trajan was then resident.

2.4 *a mathematico* Astrology was a favorite means of forecasting the future, and Hadrian was himself much interested and very skilled in it (see 16.7). His own horoscope, drawn by Antigonus of Nicaea (second or third century) has been preserved (*CCAG* VI 97 ff., see Cramer 164ff.). See Syme (14).

The future could also be told by means of omens, but the validity of omens which predict great destiny is often not recognized until many years after the event, when historical knowledge of what has occurred permits interpretation as forecasting actuality. Biography favors the reporting of prophesy by astrology or omens, particularly the appearance of the latter, for they can often appear to be so random. The author of the HA includes 59 throughout the work. Six are found in the life of Hadrian: four refer to himself (2.4, 2.8-9, 3.4-5, 3.7), two to potential successors, Fuscus and Servianus (23.3, 23.8). The subject is treated by de Kisch (2).

Ammianus (XXII 12.8) reports that Hadrian closed the Castalian spring near Antioch because the oracle had prophesied that he would become emperor and he did not want others to be given similar prophecies. It remained closed until Julian reopened it.

2.4 *Aelio Hadriano* This great uncle is otherwise unknown. He is perhaps fabricated by the author for effect.

2.5 *Traiano adoptato* This occurred in late October 97. The praetorian guard had demanded that Nerva avenge the murder of Domitian. Nerva refused, but his refusal did no good, for the guard acted on its own. This successful challenge to the *auctoritas* of the *princeps* might have proven fatal to him, had he not, surely after much deliberation and consultation, chosen to adopt the man considered Rome's outstanding general, then in

command of Germania superior. Trajan was designated *Caesar*, a
title which clearly indicated his intended succession, and nominated as *consul* to serve with Nerva from January 1. This series
of bold and, it may be presumed, largely unexpected actions restored tranquility by establishing a succession to an aged emperor
by a much younger and more vigorous man, who was highly respected
by the troops.

2.6 *ex qua festinans* The biographer produces confusion by
omitting essential detail. Trajan, after his designation, had
moved to the lower province and had appointed Servianus as his
successor in the upper (so Syme (2) 17; wrongly, 636). Why there
should have been such ill will between Hadrian and his brother-in-law, who was much his senior and now his commander, we do not
know. (See 15.8) If Hadrian had gotten into substantial debt,
Trajan must surely have known, both as his *tutor* and his recent
commander. It would appear that Servianus was invidious and
jealous, perhaps suspecting, rightly as events proved, that his
brother-in-law would be the member of the family upon whom Trajan
bestowed ever increasing responsibility, rather than upon himself.
The tale of the intentional wreck of Hadrian's carriage or chariot
bears similarity to the story of the ship intended to bring
Agrippina's death (Tac. *Ann.* XIV 3.3). But this entire passage
may well be a malicious insertion into the basic text. In spite
of any opposition and obstacles that may have existed, Hadrian
was the first to bring Trajan the news that Nerva was dead,
death occurring on January 25, 98. The news would haven taken
at least a week to reach Upper Germany; consequently, Hadrian
ended up marching along the Rhine at the height of winter. Small
wonder that Trajan esteemed him (*fuitque in amore Traiani*), but
there were also, perhaps, homosexual relations.

  McDermott (1) has recently challenged much of the information
presented in the first six sections of this chapter. He revises
the order of provinces in which Hadrian served, and denies that
any enmity existed between him and Servianus.

2.6 *beneficiarium* This was a non-commissioned military rank.
He served as an orderly or aide; his salary was probably double
regular legionary pay. See Watson 85; Webster 263-5.

2.7 *Gallo favente* This passage has been considered corrupt
since long before Mommsen's day, who altered *ei* to *et* and *Gallo*
to *alio*. Pepe claims that it makes sense as it stands. Hadrian's
relationship with Trajan was threatened by the *paedagogi puerorum*

(for reasons that can only be conjectured) and he was protected
by Gallus. Pepe identifies this Gallus as Appius Annius Trebonius
Gallus, *cos. ord.* in 108, the year when Hadrian was consul for
the first time as *suffectus*; thus Hadrian's protector in the
years preceding was honored by a consulship almost in tandem with
his "protege," the emperor's relative. This identification may
well be true, yet the problem of the text remains. What is the
subject of *defuit*? It could be *amor*, and then something is
necessary to explain the action of the *paedagogi*, or a word like
*odium*, and then clarification is required with the ablative
absolute to indicate whether Gallus supported them or Hadrian.
The latter appears more likely; one might suggest, exempli gratia,
*odium eum Gallo favente defuit*. Whatever the solution, the
sentence, if it is to be believed, offers another instance in the
modest catalogue that this chapter offers of the ups and downs
that Hadrian enjoyed and suffered in his early career; as Servianus attempted to stymie him, so here too his position was endangered by the *paedagogi*. He needed strong support from influential people. Gallus should likely be included among them.

2.8 *Vergilianas sortes* The author is rather fond of invoking
prophecy by means of consultation of the text of Vergil, but no
other ancient source indicates that this practice existed. It
may well, therefore, be nothing but fantasy; if, however, we can
give any credence to the reports, the only safe conclusion that
can be drawn is that the practice had begun no later than the
principate of Trajan, as indicated in this passage. How was the
text consulted? Either passages of the text were written on
tablets which were placed in some receptacle, with one being
shaken out, as implied here by the verb *excidit*, or the text of
the entire poem was opened at random and the passage which the
eye first fell upon was taken as prophetic; frequently in the HA
the *sortes* are given orally as *responsa*.

The lines are *Aen.* VI 808-12, referring to Numa Pompilius;
this early king, an immigrant to the royal power in the maturity
of his years, is a favorite of the author, perhaps because he
wishes to underscore the importance of age and experience in a
ruler. Yet it may be not age, since both Numa and Hadrian were
about forty at accession, but the ruling qualities exemplified
by Numa that are emphasized: *felicitas, pietas, securitas*, and
*religio*. Hadrian used Numa as an *exemplum*. See de Kisch (1),
Zoepffel.

2.8 *Sibyllinis versibus* The existence of the Sibylline books covers almost the entire history of ancient Rome. Their origin lay in the regal period, and their charge was given to the *XVviri sacris faciundis*. They were consulted only upon command of the senate, normally only in time of emergency. The collection was culled at the order of Augustus and false oracles removed. The accepted collection was then housed in his new Temple of Apollo on the Palatine. We are given no indication of any occasion when Hadrian would have had cause to consult the books. They were last consulted in 363 and burned under Stilicho.

2.9 *fano Niceforii Iovis* Antiochus IV (175-163 B.C.) had placed a statue of Zeus Nikephoros in the Temple of Zeus at Antioch. The Victory which Zeus carried was made of solid gold; it was plundered in 123/2 by Alexander II Zabinas. That it is this shrine which the author means is suggested by the close link with Apollonius of Syria, immediately following. There is no other evidence that this temple had oracular functions.

2.9 *Apollonius* This man is otherwise unknown; he may be fictitious.

2.10 *Sura* L. Licinius Sura was, perhaps, Trajan's closest associate. He too was of Spanish origin, was *cos. suff.* about 97, and was, in all likelihood, governor of Germania inferior from 98 to 101. *Epit.* 13.6 suggests that he was instrumental in Nerva's designation of Trajan as adopted son and colleague; *cuius studio (Traianus) imperium arripuerat* (whatever *arripuerat* means; normally it implies usurpation). Rewarded with second and third consulates, both ordinary, in 102 and 107, he must have died soon thereafter, and Trajan honored him with a posthumous public statue, as well as constructing public baths bearing his name on the Aventine, near his home. Hadrian was fortunate to have the support of such an influential man. See also 3.8, 3.10, and 3.11. For his career, see C. P. Jones.

2.10 *nepte per sororem Traiani* See 1.2

2.10 *Plotina* Pompeia Plotina, Trajan's wife, was probably born in Nimes (see 12.2). We know nothing of her life prior to 100, when Pliny, in the course of his *Panegyricus*, renders her extraordinary eulogy (83.4-8).

Allowance must be made for Pliny's oratorical virtuosity, but the word which seems best to describe her is *civilis*; when

she entered the imperial palace for the first time as empress,
she uttered the prayer that she leave it, whenever that occasion
should come, the same woman as she was then (Dio LXVIII 5.5).
She was honored with the title *Augusta* from as early as 100,
unofficially, but received that honor officially in 105. We do
not know if she accompanied Trajan to the Dacian wars, but she
was with him against the Parthians, and was at his side when he
died, in Selinus (Cilicia). Our author tells us that she was
instrumental in gaining the succession for Hadrian. Here, and
in subsequent references (4.1, 4.4, 4.10), the words *favente*,
*favore*, *favore*, and *factione* appear; was her influence in his
behalf strictly political or personal as well? Dio says that
she was in love with him (LXIX 1.2).

She lived on for some five years after his accession,
until 122, at the latest. She wrote him a letter, in 121, on
behalf of the school of Epicurus in Athens, requesting dispensation from the requirement that the head of the school be a
Roman citizen and speak Latin. Hadrian granted the request,
and she then reported this to the fellowship. The first letter
is in Latin, the second in Greek (Smallwood 442). Hadrian
grieved much at her death, saying that she had never asked anything of him which was improper and that therefore he had never
denied her anything (Dio LXIX 10.3a). She was not only honored
by the basilica at Nimes but became joint dedicatee of the
great temple that Hadrian built to Trajan to complete the huge
forum of Trajan; this was the only building or monument for which
Hadrian was in any way responsible upon which he put his own
name. The dedicatory inscription concludes with the words
*parentibus suis*, thereby confirming his adoption (*ILS* 306).
Coins similarly confirm that she became a *diva*. See also 9.9

2.10 *Marius Maximus*   L. Marius Maximus Perpetuus Aurelianus had
a long and distinguished career of public service and continued
Suetonius' *De Vita Caesarum* with a dozen lives of his own, from
Nerva to Elagabalus, not including a life of Verus. He was
governor of Belgica, Germania inferior, Syria Coele, and Dacia,
*consul suffectus* in 198 or 199, *proconsul* of Asia in 214-15 and
again in 218-20, *praefectus urbi* in 217/8, and *proconsul* of
Africa in 221/22. His career was crowned with a second consulate
as *ordinarius* in 223. He played an important role in Septimius
Severus' rise to power and his consolidation of it and was a
major and trusted associate of Caracalla.

He thus falls into the Roman pattern of history being written by senators, men who had participated in and witnessed the workings of government. Dio Cassius, his contemporary, followed this same course. But Maximus chose not to write the history of his age or the period of the Antonines preceding it, but rather to compose imperial biographies. He seems to have had a prediliction for the fanciful and the scandalous, using the *acta urbis* as a main source. He is cited more than two dozen times by the author of the HA, whence Peter took entries for his *HRR* (II 121-29). He is described as a tedious and unreliable author: *homo omnium verbosissimus, qui et mythistoricis se voluminibus inplicavit* (*Quad. Tyr.* 1.2).

The great problem in HA source studies is whether Maximus was the main (or, occasionally, only) source for the author or merely subsidiary, used to embellish an otherwise sober and factual account, whose author can be dubbed *Ignotus*. At present there is no scholarly consensus, although the scales seem to be tilting toward the primacy of *Ignotus*.

He is cited as a source in three other places in the *Vita*, all unfavorable to Hadrian: 12.4, 20.3, 25.4.

3.1 *Quaesturam* The year was 101. Hadrian was one of the emperor's quaestors, the *quaestores Caesaris*.

3.1 *agrestius pronuntians* Where did Hadrian pick up his peculiar accent, for that is what the text must refer to? If he spent much of his youth in Rome and no more than two or three years in Italica, it may be that the *urbanitas* of the capital was destroyed by the local speech in his mid-teens. But that seems unlikely. Yet one need not conclude that he indeed lived in Spain for much of his childhood. He could have heard Spanish accent and intonation in his home from servants and slaves. See 1.5

3.2 *acta senatus* The *acta senatus* were the official record of proceedings, motions, speeches, votes, and decisions of the senate during the empire. These *acta* were housed in the *secretarium senatus* adjacent to the *curia* and were available for consultation by any senator. The magistrate in charge was usually at an early stage of his senatorial career, and, at least from the reign of Tiberius, was chosen by the emperor (Tac. *Ann.* V 4. 1: *Iunius Rusticus, componendis patrum actis delectus a Caesare.*).

3.2 *bellum Dacicum*   This was the first war, 101-102.

3.3 *indulsisse vino*   For Trajan's *vinolentia*, cf. *Epit.* 13.4: *tantus erat in eo maximarum rerum modus, ut quasi temperamento quodam virtutes miscuisse videretur, nisi quod cibo vinoque paululum deditus erat.*

3.4 *Candido et Quadrato iterum conss.*   105 is the year; both held second consulates.

3.5 *tribuniciam potestatem*   The gradual development of the Augustan principate ultimately gave Augustus two main sources of power, the consular and proconsular *imperium* and the tribunician power. Augustus speaks frequently enough, in the *Res Gestae*, of the former, and it was very visible, for it vested in him the command of armies and the government of provinces. But the *tribunicia potestas* was not quite as visible. Only by stages, in 36, 30, and finally 23 B.C., did Augustus obtain all the powers of the republican *tribunus plebis*, and indeed more, without the need to hold the office and without any real limitation of tenure, even though the senate voted him this power for five and ten year periods. The tribunician power was renewed each year, and the change in its number was the only effective means of dating, since consulates and imperatorial acclamations did not automatically change with the year. Tac. *Ann.* III 56.2 acutely spoke of the *tribunicia potestas* as *summi fastigii vocabulum*.

3.5 *paenulas*   This notice is inaccurate. The normal raincoat in the age of Trajan was the *lacerna*; nevertheless, the *paenula*, earlier ordinary weather clothing for all ranks below the senatorial order, now became common for senators as well. It is clear, from representations of Trajan on his column, that he wore it while on campaign, and it must have served as well as a travel garment. The normal imperial military garment was the *paludamentum*, but the *paenula* would have been worn over it. Hadrian must have worn it extensively on his journeys. See Wilson 87-92 (*paenula*), 100-4 (*paludamentum*), who describes the former (89) as "a heavy cloak for cold and rainy weather, and . . . made of either heavy, shaggy woolen cloth or of leather," Kolb and Alföldi 124-8. See also 2.4

3.5 *unde hodieque*   This can only refer to the period in which the author is writing. In earlier days, the emperor was not distinguished from others by his dress; part of his wardrobe

embraced *privata vestis*. But in late antiquity, when the
emperor's position was in every respect different from that of
ordinary citizens, his clothing differed too. Since the *paenula*
had become the normal costume of citizens and above all senators,
no longer being limited particularly to foul weather, the emperor
ceased to wear it. This suits the latter part of the fourth
century.

3.6 *secunda expeditione Dacica*   105-106.

3.6 *primae legioni Minerviae*   This legion was raised by Domitian
in 83 and given the name of his patron divinity. Its headquarters
was Bonn. It participated in his German campaigns, and Trajan
became familiar with its quality when he was governor of Germania
inferior. It fought in the first Dacian war, was then stationed
in the conquered land, and fought again in the second, with
Hadrian as *legatus legionis*. He held this post simultaneously
with the praetorship (106), and was rewarded by Trajan with the
*dona militaria*, as he had already been in the first war, if we
may so interpret part of the famous Athens inscription (see App.
II): *donis militaribus ab eo donato bis*. The legion returned
to Bonn in 107.

3.7 *adamante gemma*   On the omen, see 2.4

3.8 *Subsurano bis et Serviano iterum conss.* The text is corrupt
and the historical information thus confused. A *Subsuranus* does
not appear in the consular fasti in this period. To read *sub
Surano* is to produce jargon, not Latin; *Suburano* will clear away
this difficulty. Sex. Attius Suburanus Aemilianus was *cos. II*
in 104; L. Iulius Ursus Servianus *cos. II* in 102. Neither date
is possible, for the tribunate of the people did not come until
105. But L. Licinius Sura was *cos. III* in 107, with Q. Sosius
Senecio, *cos. II*, as colleague. This must be the year referred
to; hence read *Sura tertium et Senecione iterum conss*. See 4.2.
But even this solution does not eliminate error, for Hadrian's
praetorship fell in 106. Hadrian moved from the tribunate to the
praetorship without a break. This is anomalous, and may be the
cause for our author's error. See App. II.

3.8 *iterum*   A difficult word. If it bears its accustomed meaning,
we are then at a loss concerning the first occasion when the
emperor gave Hadrian money for games. That interpretation makes
little sense. Does it mean that Trajan gave the money in two

equal installments, so that *iterum vicies* is the equivalent of
*quadragies*? That is better, but still not very satisfying.
Perhaps Mommsen's deletion is the best response.

3.8 *ludos* Under the republic, the *cura ludorum* had been the
responsibility of the aediles, who were able to gain great public
favor by their extravagance, as well as contract enormous debts.
Augustus transferred this responsibility to the praetors in 22
B.C., and it became one of their chief duties as their legal
responsibilities were increasingly diminished. This was one of
the aspects of Agricola's praetorship that Tacitus particularly
mentioned (*Agr.* 6.4): *ludos et inania honoris medio rationis
atque abundantiae duxit, uti longe a luxuria ita famae propior.*

3.9 *legatus* There is no external evidence for a war against
the Sarmatians in 107-8. It is likely that the author is doing
no more than retailing the qualities of a good governor: suitable
protection of his province, maintenance of the military discipline
upon which that protection depended, and supervision, as far as
possible, of the procurators, whose concern was financial. For
an earlier expression of the hatred which the latter could arouse,
see Tac. *Agr.* 15.2.

3.10 *Sura* See 2.10

3.10 *adoptandum se* The year is 108, in all likelihood the year
in which Sura died. If he did report news of impending adoption
to Hadrian, the event proved him mistaken, for adoption did not
occur until Trajan was on his deathbed, if indeed, as gossip
indicated, even then. It may be that Sura's death was responsible
for Trajan's failure to take a step he was contemplating. Sura
may well have been pushing the (seemingly obvious) suitability
of his fellow "Spaniard."

The words *adoptandum esse* serve here as a future passive
infinitive, rather than the classical gerundive use of necessity
or obligation.

3.11 *dictaverat* Evidently because of the great fluency that
Hadrian had developed a few years before (3.1), which, with his
interest in literature, made him perhaps the most "literary" of
all emperors. Nero was the first emperor who used the eloquence
of another; we do not know of the practice of his successors
before Trajan, but it seems likely that they continued to do so.
Tac. *Ann.* XIII 3 comments upon the oratorical abilities of the

first four Julio-Claudians. Note how this chapter begins and concludes with references to his oral performance and duties.

**4.1** *Plotinae* See 2.10

**4.1** *legatus* We do not know precisely what function Hadrian filled as *legatus* during the first years of the Parthian War. He had already been a legionary commander in 106 and governor of a major province, Pannonia inferior, in 107. He could hardly have held a post less important. Perhaps he served on Trajan's staff as *comes* before his appointment as governor of Syria, which came no later than July 117.

**4.2** *Sosi Papi* Such a man does not exist. Read *Sosi [Senecionis, Aemili] Papi*. For the former, much is known; for the latter, very little. He appears in *CIL* XIV 3516 in a dedication to a deceased son. See Pflaum (4).

Q. Sosius Senecio had a meteoric career under Domitian and Trajan, with military distinctions in both Dacian Wars and two consulates, both ordinary. He was one of only three men to whom Trajan granted the honor of a public statue while still alive. There is no mention of him in the *Vita Hadriani*, save in this garbled form. See C. P. Jones, whose first paragraph reads: "At first glance, L. Licinius Sura and Q. Sosius Senecio have many points of resemblance. Both were men of erudition and culture, like their mutual friend the younger Pliny. Both stood close to Trajan and participated in the two Dacian wars. Both received the rare honour of a public statue from the emperor. Together they gave their names to the year 107, sharing the *fasces* as *consules ordinarii*."

**4.2** *Platori Nepotis* Suffect consul in 119, with the emperor as his colleague, he was sent out that same year as governor of Germania inferior, from which province he moved, in 122, to Britannia. He may well have accompanied Hadrian on the latter's tour of the island province, and have stood with him when the decision was made, in Northumberland and Cumberland, to build a great wall along the northern frontier of the empire to control movement across that frontier. Building stones from the Wall recall the construction and his tenure: *Imp. Caes. Traian. Hadriani Aug. leg. II Aug. A. Platorio Nepote leg. pr. pr.* (Smallwood 319). Legio II Augusta had its permanent fortress at Caerleon; it, along with legio XX Valeria Victrix from Chester and legio VI Victrix from York, sent detachments to accomplish the technically difficult tasks of engineering and construction.

We do not know any details of Nepos' career after his governorship of Britain; he may even have died in Britain. For a dedicatory inscription from Aquileia, of which he was *patronus*, see Smallwood 229.

Here his friendship is said to have been useful to Hadrian at the time of the *expeditio Parthica*. Yet, in 15.2, he is one of those whom Hadrian subsequently *hostium loco habuit*. No known details confirm the last statement.

4.2 *Attiani* See 1.4 and 15.2

4.2 *Liviani* Ti. Claudius Livianus, whose full, polyonymous name, Ti. Iulius Aquilinus Castricius Saturninus Claudius Livianus, bespeaks adoption. He was praetorian prefect early in Trajan's reign and during the first Dacian war was sent on an embassy to Decebalus in company with Licinius Sura. We do not know how long he held the prefecture, but he had been supplanted before the death of Trajan.

4.2 *Turbonis* His full name is Q. Marcius Turbo Fronto Publicius Severus. He had an extraordinary career, in some respects unparalleled; the following offices are known, along with their dates, certain or conjectural.

> *primipilus in Aquincum* (?) c. 104-5
> *praefectus vehiculorum*   before 107
> *tribunus cohortis VII vigilum*        between 107-8
> *tribunus equitum singularium Augusti*    and
> *tribunus praetorianus*                110-12
> *primipilus II*
> *procurator ludi magni*   c. 112-3
> *praefectus classis praetoriae Misenensis*   113-4
> command against the Jews in Egypt and Cyrenaica (*pro legato*?)   116-7
> *procurator Mauretaniae* (*Caesariensis*?)   117-8
> special command in Pannonia inferior and Dacia (*pro legato*?)   118-23 (?)
> *praefectus praetorio*   123 (?)--

A recently found diploma (*AE* 1973, 459) reveals Turbo as being in command in Pannonia in 123, which means that the praetorian prefecture cannot be earlier than that year.

The office *tribunus praetorianus*, if that is the correct expansion of the abbreviation and not *praetoriorum*, suggests that

he received the rank without receiving the office and carrying
out its duties. It would thus be an honorary promotion. His
command along the Danube was quite remarkable, for it was normally a consular post. He was responsible for the reorganization
of Dacia into two provinces, *superior* and *inferior*. In 7.3, he
is said to have been *ornatus titulo Aegyptiacae praefecturae*;
does this mean that he also held the prefecture of Egypt, perhaps
*in absentia*? This does not seem likely; his status was undoubtedly meant to be the equal of that of the prefect of Egypt, in
other words, at the very top of the equestrian *cursus*. See
Pflaum (1) #94; Syme (4).

Dio LXIX 18 offers a splendid report on his ability and
devotion to duty.

4.3 *adoptionis sponsionem Sponsio* is a legal term that implies
a formal agreement; Paulus describes it as *omnis stipulatio
promissioque*. As such, its significance is far greater than
the *praesumptio* mentioned in 4.4 which followed it. If indeed
Trajan never formally adopted Hadrian, he may have indicated an
intention to do so, reserving the legal formalities until his
return to Rome.

4.3 *Palma* A. Cornelius Palma Frontonianus was one of Trajan's
chief associates, as shown by his two consulates, both of them
ordinary. The first was in 99, and he then became legate of Hispania Tarraconensis, his tenure lasting from 99/100 to 101/2.
From 104/5 to 107/8, he was legate of the immensely important
province of Syria; in 106 he reduced the Arabs of Nabataea and
brought that part of Arabia into the empire. For this achievement, he was honored with the *ornamenta triumphalia* and a public
statue, and in 109 entered upon his second consulate. We know
of no subsequent office, but it does not seem likely that Trajan
would have permitted a man of his distinction to remain in retirement during the Parthian War. Nor do we know why he and
Hadrian became hostile toward each other.

His origin was probably Italian, perhaps Volsinii in
Etruria. Tarracina, where he met his death, is the modern
Terracina, situated on the western coast of Italy approximately
half way between Rome and Naples. Trajan had been responsible
for major harbor and road works in that city, thereby making
the route of the Via Appia easier and more direct. Is there perhaps some connection between Palma and the city, so that we may
conjecture that he was instrumental in the imperial works carried
on here?

Commentary                                                            59

4.3 *Celso* In spite of clear eminence and importance, L. Publilius Celsus is almost unknown. He was twice consul (*suff.* in 102, *ord.* in 113), the last man under Trajan to receive an iterated consulate, and he was also honored by a triumphal statue. But what provinces he governed and in what war (or wars) he fought cannot be stated. He is here joined with Palma in long-standing enmity toward Hadrian.

Baiae is the renowned spa on the Bay of Naples.

4.3 *in suspicionem adfectatae tyrannidis* We know nothing of any such attempt; it may be fictional.

4.4 *Plotinae* See 2.10

4.4 *factus* This is wrong; it should be *designatus*. But the distinction may be too literal. The verb *facio* is common, when the emperor appointed the consuls: see 3.10 and 8.4.

4.4 *praesumptionem adoptionis emeruit* See 4.3 and 2.9

4.5 *corrupisse . . . curasse . . . inisse* An odd and totally unexpected intrusion, personal slander disturbing the orderly narrative of Hadrian's political fortunes. Trajan's fondness for young men was well-known in antiquity, yet only his passion for drink was remembered centuries later (see 3.3). Nowhere does the author of the *vita* pass full judgment upon Trajan, but the impression is given of a man who has personal vices and is too much influenced by his wife and other female relations. He evidently was not much in favor of Hadrian's marriage with his grandniece Sabina (2.10).

4.6 *legatus Suriae* The most significant post in the emperor's service at the time, with the war against Parthia still underway and various revolts rending the east. A substantial part of the military strength of the empire was in his hands, now that Trajan had started on the journey back to Rome; there were, at the minimum, eleven legions with additional support. See 6.2

4.6 *litteras adoptionis* This statement indicates that Trajan adopted Hadrian some days before his death, since one must allow a minimum of two days for the letter to be delivered to Syria. Vict. *Caes.* 13.11 supports this: *ascito prius ad imperium Hadriano civi propinquoque*. If so, then the rumor that the adoption was never made while Trajan was alive, but was fraudulently accomplished through the influence of Plotina (4.10),

cannot be correct. Yet Dio reports that Hadrian had not been
adopted, and succeeded because he was nearby and controlled a
large army (LXIX 1.1-2). It is perhaps an odd coincidence that
M. Ulpius Phaedimus, Trajan's freedman, died on August 12, and was
buried in Selinus; his remains were removed to Rome only in 130.
Some might have suspected poison. See Smallwood 176.

4.7 *natalem imperii* His first tribunician power began on this
date, and lasted only until December 10, the traditional republican date when the tribunes entered upon their office. *Dies
imperii* is more commonly used than *natalis imperii*. His second
year of tribunician power thus ran from December 10, 117, to
December 9, 118.

Thus Nerva, in barely sixteen months of rule, had three
years of tribunician power: from his *dies imperii*, September 18,
96, to December 9, 96, from December 10 to December 9, 97, and
then to his death on January 25, 98.

4.8 *id animi* A partitive genitive, routinely used after neuter
adjectives and pronouns.

4.8 *Neratium Priscum* This man was an eminent jurist, suffect
consul in 97, but without any marked recommendation for the
principate. He was not a soldier, and Trajan had not even
honored him with a second consulate. This report must be fiction,
as is the following report that Trajan intended to leave the
choice of a successor to the senate. Had he done so, with a
favored list of candidates, a peaceful succession would have been
impossible, for the rejected hopefuls could hardly have expected
to remain alive. The choice of the best man by the senate
smacks of Galba's speech on the adoption of Piso Licinianus in
Tac. *Hist.* I 15-16.

He is mentioned in 18.1 for his legal eminence. The Marcellus of 15.4 is probably his brother. For his career, see Syme
(1).

4.9 *exemplo Alexandri* Alexander the Great died in Babylon in
323, in his thirty-third year. He had conquered a vast empire,
but his sudden final illness prevented him, if indeed he had the
desire to do so, from choosing one from his numerous associates
to succeed him. Perhaps he could not have done so even had he
wished, for among the Macedonians the army chose the king. But
his decease was followed by rivalries and warfare among his
generals, who carved out individual monarchies for themselves,

until, at the last, after some two score years, the political
pattern of the Hellenistic world was set, with the three major
kingdoms of the Antigonids, the Seleucids, and the Ptolemies, as
well as a few small independent monarchies such as Pergamum.

4.10   *Plotinae*   See 2.10

4.10   *adoptionem*   See 4.6

5.1   *priscum . . . morem*   The precedent is Augustan. In his
final instructions to his successor, Augustus had urged the
*consilium coercendi intra terminos imperii* (Tac. *Ann.* I 11.4),
and the greatest achievement of his principate was the *pax
Augusta*, commemorated by the most significant of Augustan monuments, the *ara pacis Augustae*. Alexander the Great had been
Trajan's model; there was a vast psychological difference between
the two.

5.2   *nationibus*   Assyria, Armenia, Mesopotamia.

5.2   *Mauri lacessebant*   Mauretania, brought into the empire as
a province by Gaius, was a source of constant trouble for the
Romans, challenging the peace of both Numidia to the east and
the Spanish provinces across the Strait of Gibraltar. Suetonius
Paulinus led an army against the Moors in 41; during this campaign he became the first Roman to cross the Atlas Mountains and
wrote a book about this experience. But troubles continued
intermittently. See 12.7

5.2   *Sarmatae*   See 6.6

5.2   *Brittanni*   See 11.2. Contemporary testimony to the up-
risings of the Moors and the Britons comes from Juvenal (XIV
196):
   *dirue Maurorum attegias, castella Brigantum*

5.2   *Aegyptus seditionibus urgebatur*   This was an uprising of
the Jews, which began in Cyrenaica and spread eastward. The
prefect of Egypt being unable to quell the revolt fully, Trajan
assigned the task to Turbo (see 5.8 and 9.4), who accomplished it
with great vigor. How great the threat to the stability of
Egypt, and the empire, was can be seen from the need for rein-
forcements which an Egyptian cohort on duty in 117 had; in 126,
recruits from Asia were assigned to it. "Whatever the details,
the cohort's need for so many replacements and the fact that

they were brought in from another province are impressive
evidence for the serious and bloody nature of the Jewish revolt
in Egypt, and serve to illustrate one of the many problems that
Hadrian faced at his accession." (Gilliam [1]) The Jews were
probably supported by the Egyptian peasants. Egypt, Libya, and
Palestine were all linked in the Jewish war. See Fuks.

5.2 *Libya* This is generally considered the part of north Africa
between the provinces of Africa and Egypt. Libya was not established as an independent province until 297; the name is surely
late Latin for Cyrenaica.

5.2 *Palaestina* Palestine had been annexed, along with Samaria
and Idumaea, under Augustus; the three regions constituted the
province of Judaea and were governed by a procurator. After the
great rebellion of 66-70, the governor was an imperial legate of
praetorian rank. The revolt mentioned here was part of the
Jewish uprising which began in 115 (see above) and spread eastward from Cyrenaica as far as Mesopotamia. It was really a revolt of the diaspora. Lusius Quietus crushed the revolt in
Judaea (see 5.8) in 117. Palestine is not to be distinguished
from Judaea. At some time in the 120s, Judaea received a second
legion on permanent station, and was thereafter governed by a
legate of consular rank.

5.3 *omnia* The peoples mentioned at the beginning of the previous sentence. Hadrian, with the east in flames at his accession, realized that the empire's resources were inadequate to
control so vast and so distant an area. He showed, in years to
come, that he favored a defensive posture, protected, where
possible, by natural barriers such as rivers and mountains or
by artificial ones such as the wall in Britain and *limites* elsewhere (see 11.2 and 12.6). It was also thought that he intended
to abandon Dacia, but was dissuaded (Eutr. VIII 6.2): *Idem de
Dacia facere conatum amici deterruerunt, ne multi cives Romani
barbaris traderentur, propterea quia Traianus victa Dacia ex
toto orbe Romano infinitas eo copias hominum transtulerat ad
agros et urbes colendas.*

5.3 *Catonis* The eminent M. Porcius Cato Censorius. This speech
was delivered in 167 B.C., after the victory of L. Aemilius
Paullus over Perseus. Livy's report (XLV 18.1-2) may well be
based upon Cato's own words, of which only one pathetic fragment
survives (Malcovati *ORF* XLI).

5.4 *Parthamasirin* This should be Parthamaspates. He was made king of the client state Osroene after his removal from the throne of Parthia. See 13.8, 21.10

5.5 *clementiae* This is one of the standard imperial virtues, beginning with the famed--and, by many, bitterly resented-- *clementia Caesaris*. The *clupeus virtutis* granted Augustus by decree of the senate in 27 B.C. commemorated his *virtus, clementia, iustitia*, and *pietas*, and it, this second virtue, was a regular slogan on the coinage. For an actual instance of Hadrian's clemency, but not in a political sense, which was the norm, see 12.5.

5.5 *sub primis imperii diebus* Attianus wrote from Rome, so that the immediacy of his action should not be taken too literally. Some time will, of necessity, have passed.

5.5 *Attiano* See 1.4 and 15.2

5.5 *Baebius Macer* Not a great deal is known about his career, and some of the details here presented are by no means certainly linked with him. He was an orator and a friend of Pliny, *curator viae Appiae* about 95, and proconsul of Baetica 100/1. He succeeded to a suffect consulship in 103. When his tenure as *praefectus urbi* began is unknown; he must have enjoyed Trajan's favor, since the prefecture was particularly important with the emperor away from Rome, and he might well have been rewarded with a second consulate had Trajan lived. Evidently Baebius did not oppose any obstacles to Hadrian's succession, but he seems nonetheless to have been removed from his post. When and how he died are unknown.

5.5 *Laberius Maximus* An Italian from Lanuvium, he was the only one of Trajan's marshals to lose the emperor's favor. He was suffect consul in 89, governor of Moesia inferior from 100-2, at the beginning of the first Dacian war, and performed exemplary feats in that campaign. He took a fortified town by storm and captured the sister of King Decebalus. His reward followed in the year 103, when he was *cos. II ordinarius*, with the emperor as colleague. What his actions were which caused him to be *suspectus imperio* is unknown, as is the date of his relegation. Hadrian certainly did not put him to death; but he probably did not recall him, and we do not know the date or the circumstances of his death.

His full name is M.' Laberius Maximus Quintius (or Marcius) Crispinus.

**5.5** *Frugi Crassus* His full name was C. Calpurnius Crassus Frugi Licinianus; he was a scion of two distinguished families which reached back to the heyday of the republic, the Calpurnii Pisones Frugi and the Licinii Crassi. Suffect consul in 87, he conspired against Nerva and was relegated to Tarentum; recalled by Trajan, he again conspired against the emperor and was again relegated, this time to an island. Hadrian did not put him to death at his accession, but was spared the possibility of a third conspiracy on Crassus' part by the procurator's action. His ancestry might well have given him illusions of grandeur, causing him to think himself a worthier princeps than an elderly senator or a Spaniard, and clearly made him a formidable potential rival. For discussion of the families, see Syme (3).

**5.7** *auspicia imperii* From the earliest days of Rome's history, indeed from the contest between Romulus and Remus to determine the name of the new city, it was deemed essential to discover the will of the gods before any significant undertaking. The taking of the auspices was one of the means of maintaining the *pax deorum*. Only a magistrate with *imperium* could take the *auspicia* during the republic; in the principate, this right--and power--belonged to the emperor alone.

Immediately after Hadrian had received the news of Trajan's death (see 4.7), he would have been hailed as *imperator* by the army and would then have taken the auspices, to ascertain whether he had heaven's support. The largess then followed.

**5.7** *largitionem* Coins give evidence of seven *liberalitates*. Hadrian's first, given in his absence, was three *aurei* per person, the equivalent of 75 denarii. This, the second, was *duplex*, hence 150 denarii. The third one (see 7.3) was similar. If we assume that the remaining distributions were of the same order, then the total for the reign was 39 *aurei*; perhaps the last, in honor of his adoption of Ceionius Commodus, who became Aelius Caesar, was even larger, and if it were seven *aurei* the sum will be 40 (see 23.12). This total of 1000 *denarii*, which equals 4000 sesterces, compares with Augustus' distribution of 362 1/2 *denarii* during his long reign and Trajan's 650. This substantial total was only surpassed by Septimius Severus. See Mattingly (1) and, for a somewhat different sequence, van Berchem 152-4.

5.8 *Lusium Quietum* A Moorish chieftain, Lusius Quietus served under Domitian, probably along the Danube, as commander of native cavalry and was subsequently dismissed in disgrace. Trajan recalled him to service in the first Dacian War when the emperor required the assistance of the Moors; Lusius displayed great personal valor, slew many of the enemy, was honored for his actions, and achieved even greater distinction in the second war. During the Parthian War, he reached the height of renown and success (the following dates are not fully secure):

  114 he defeated the Mardi
  115 he captured Singara and other towns without a battle
  116 in the revolt of Mesopotamia, he recaptured Nisibis and destroyed Edessa
  117 he exterminated the Jews who had revolted in Mesopotamia
  117 appointed *legatus Augusti pro praetore* of Judaea, he waged a vicious war against the Jews
    (at some time between the beginning of the war and his appointment to Judaea, he was adlected into the senate *inter praetorios*)
 c.117 *consul suffectus*
  117 discharged by Hadrian, after his Moorish cavalry were removed and he was thereby rendered helpless
  118 he was killed on a trip, perhaps returning home to Mauretania

No ancient source explains Hadrian's enmity toward him, if enmity did indeed exist. The new emperor may have felt that a general as cruel and effective as Lusius in the extirpation of enemies had no role to play in his foreign policy, one of retrenchment and, where possible, peaceful relations.

5.8 *Mauris* These were Lusius' personal bodyguard. They were ordered to abandon their prince and to return to Mauretania. The *tumultus* followed, perhaps instigated by them.

5.8 *Marcio Turbone* See 4.2

5.9 *Antiochia* See 14.1

5.9 *Attianus* See 1.4 and 15.2

5.9 *Plotina* See 2.10

5.9 *Matidia* Trajan's niece, Hadrian's mother-in-law. See 9.9

5.10 *exceptis* = "receiving them in audience;" perhaps there is also the sense of "having caught up with them," although they were not at that point travelling, waiting at Selinus.

5.10 *Catilio Severo*  Did Hadrian hand over his province immediately upon receipt of the news that he had succeeded Trajan or only after he had returned to Antioch, after he had paid his respects to Trajan's remains? The text does not enable us to be sure; probably it was the former, which would put Catilius in command in August 117.

L. Catilius Severus was a man of great distinction, who reached the highest levels of a senatorial career. Consul for the first time in 110, and thus probably of about the same age as Hadrian, he was one of Trajan's marshals, being governor of the two Armenias and Cappadocia between 114 and 117. Hadrian, immediately after his accession to the principate, chose him as his own successor as governor of Syria. He was consul for the second time in 120, with the future Antoninus Pius as colleague, governor of Africa about 124/25, and *praefectus urbi*. If indeed he was discovered to have aspired to the succession, and had taken steps to accomplish this, he would seem to have been driven by pride and ambition rather than by a sense of reality, for his age should have clearly eliminated him even from his own deliberations. But he was related to Marcus, evidently by marriage: perhaps he was step-great-grandfather. The young Marcus, early in life, bore the name Catilius Severus, from his *maternus proavus* (MA 1.9).

It may be that Hadrian's enmity toward him (15.7) is connected with his disappointment at Antoninus' preference.

5.10 *Romam venit*  This sequence telescopes time terribly. Hadrian will have caught up with Attianus, Plotina, and Matidia certainly still in August, returned at once, still in that month or September, to Antioch, and have stayed there, consolidating his administration, through the autumn and perhaps the early part of winter. The land journey through Illyricum bespeaks winter travel, when the sea was, if possible, avoided. There seems to be a doublet with 7.3.

On January 3, the Arval Brethren meet *votorum nuncupandorum causa pro salute imp.* etc.; clearly Hadrian is not in Rome. No earlier than June 8, perhaps as late as July 10 (the date is VI Idus of an unidentified month, because of a lacuna), the Brethren make sacrifice *ob adventum* of the emperor, who is himself present for the ceremony. It is thus likely that Hadrian was away from Rome for almost eleven months after he succeeded. This seems an extremely long time, although there was a precedent for such a leisurely arrival in Trajan's absence for more than a year after his succession. See Smallwood 6.

6.1 *divinos honores* The deification of the beloved emperor was a foregone conclusion. We do not know the details of Hadrian's request, nor what additional honors the senate decreed on its own. Games were celebrated in honor of his consecration, and we must assume that a *flamen* and *sodales* were appointed to perform the duties of the cult of *divus Traianus*, but no evidence exists for them (see 27.2-3).

Trajan's ashes were placed in the base of his column, within the boundary of the city proper, a distinction which none of his predecessors had had. Still in the fourth century, his memory was so green that the senate acclaimed a new emperor with the cry, *Felicior Augusto, melior Traiano* (Eutr. VIII 5.3).

6.1 *accuratissimis litteris* "a very carefully composed letter"

6.2 *de imperio suo* Hadrian was, of course, in Syria when Trajan died; he rightly said that it would have been intolerable for the empire to be without a head for the weeks necessary for the senate to confer *imperium* formally, particularly during an important military campaign. Yet, before he returned to Rome and had been formally invested with *imperium* by the senate, he was recognized by several cities of the East as Trajan's successor, and *P. Giss.* 3 has preserved a remarkable text. "Shortly after October 117, the consecration of the deceased Emperor Trajan and the accession of his successor were celebrated at *Heptakomia*, the metropolis of the Egyptian nome *Apollonopolites*. The papyrus seems to be an official draft for the celebration. Phoebus himself appears on the stage and proclaims in highly poetic language:

"'Having just mounted aloft with Trajan in my chariot of white horses, I come to you, oh people, I, Phoebus, by no means an unknown god, to proclaim the new ruler Hadrian, whom all things serve on account of his virtue and the genius of his divine father.'" (Alexander 143; text also in Smallwood 519)

Trajan was not officially consecrated until 118, in Rome. His acceptance among the *divi* so soon after his death certainly made Hadrian's succession a bit more secure, at least in the

east. That there was some opposition in the west appears clear
from the "conspiracy" of the four consulars (7.1-3).

That there might have been a return to the old republic
without an emperor was no longer considered even a remote possibility, after the events of 68-9 and 96-7. The only hope that
the state possessed was that the new ruler be the best available.
See 4.9

6.2 *sine imperatore* For this view, cf. Tac. *Hist.* I 16.1:
*Si immensum imperii corpus stare ac librari sine rectore posset,
dignus eram a quo res publica inciperet: nunc eo necessitatis
iam pridem ventum est, ut nec mea senectus conferre plus populo
Romano possit quam bonum successorem, nec tua plus iuventa quam
bonum principem.* The speaker is Galba, addressing Piso Licinianus; it does not take much imagination to picture Trajan saying
that to Hadrian. See 4.9

It was, of course, essential that the Roman army have a
commander-in-chief, else the opportunity for provincial governors
to claim the throne for themselves could have produced a period
of civil war comparable to that of 68-9. The army consisted of
thirty legions at the time of Trajan's death; it is impossible to
determine the disposition of all of them, but it seems that
eleven, with detachments from other legions and from auxiliary
units, were involved in the Parthian War. As governor of Syria,
Hadrian already held the most important military command.

6.3 *cum triumphum* There seems to be no reason to doubt that
Hadrian carried out this triumph for Trajan. But Trajan's consecration   probably was a separate ceremony; the funeral proces-
sion mentioned in *Epit.* 13.11 should not be conflated. See den
Boer (2); Smallwood 54.

6.3 *optimus imperator* Trajan had been called *optimus princeps*
unofficially as early as 100, and the adjective became part of his
official titulature by 114.

6.4 *patris patriae nomen* This title was the last element of
Augustus' official titulature, which he obtained in the year 2
B.C. Tiberius never received (or wanted) it at all, and subsequent emperors, down to the end of the second century, waited a
decent interval after accession before accepting it. Thus Hadrian
is following an accepted precedent, which linked him, as it had
others, with Augustus. He took the title in 128, on the birthday

of Rome, April 21, a holiday long celebrated as the Parilia but now important in conjunction with his great Temple of Venus and Rome.

Nonetheless, coins and inscriptions of the period immediately following his succession contain the title *p.p.* He had not yet had the opportunity to make his feelings known to the people and the bureaucracy. See Smallwood 110, 111.

6.5 *aurum coronarium* The practice of offering victorious generals gold crowns had its origin in the East, and became common in the last two centuries of the republic. Under the principate, communities made such gifts only to the emperor, on all important occasions, going far beyond military triumphs. Such irregular "gifts" to the emperor became a significant burden upon the communities of the empire. Sums of money routinely replaced the original crowns. Such subvention to the treasury at Rome could be welcome at times of financial stringency. Hadrian, in an act of obsequious generosity, although the *aerarium* was in desperate straits, refused the accustomed gift on the occasion of his accession from Italy and accepted only a part from the provinces. How much can perhaps be inferred from *AP* 4.10: *aurum coronarium . . . Italicis totum, medium provincialibus reddidit.* For an example of the inability of a city to make this contribution, see Smallwood 449 (b).

6.6 *tumultu Sarmatarum et Roxalanorum* Two people or one? If two, then the Sarmatae were, in all likelihood, the Iazyges, who inhabited a salient pointing southward between the provinces of Pannonia and Dacia, and the Roxolani lived to their east, southeast of Dacia. That makes sense, from what is known of Marcius Turbo's career (see 4.2), who had a special command in Pannonia and Dacia. The strategy would have called for a pincer movement against the Sarmatae from the two provinces, while the Roxolani would have been attacked directly from the south. But no conclusion of a war against the Sarmatae is recorded, and Hadrian settled the dispute against the Roxolani by diplomacy (see 6.8). This king may be the man known later as P. Aelius Rasparaganus, soon found resident in Pola, on the Istrian peninsula. His son is P. Aelius Peregrinus (the cognomen is suggestive). In one inscription he is *rex Roxolanorum*, in the other *rex Sarmatarum* (*ILS* 852, 853). Here is perhaps the key. The difficulty that faced Hadrian was with only one people, not two; since the Roxolani were a Sarmatian tribe, our author was led astray. Rasparaganus, who had agreed to help protect the frontier of the Roman

province for pay (*stipendia*, 6.8), complained over the reduction
of that pay, threatened war, and was mollified by direct consultation with Hadrian. The emperor then removed him from his king-
ship and allowed him to live out his life in Pola, and the king
took a Roman name with the emperor's *praenomen* and *nomen*, or, it
may be, his own people expelled him in dissatisfaction with the
outcome of negotiations.

6.7 *Marcium Turbonem*   See 4.2

6.7 *praefecturae infulis*   An *infula* was a woolen fillet, worn
upon the forehead, first limited to religious functions, worn
both by sacrificial animals and by priests. Later *infulae* served
also as insignia of office, as here.

6.7 *Daciae*   Eutr. VIII 6.2 reports that Hadrian intended to
abandon Dacia as well as the eastern provinces, and was only
dissuaded by his friends, *ne multi cives Romani barbaris traderentur*. It seems a fantastic thought, which should be discounted.
Dacia had been conquered more than a decade earlier, and had
been extensively settled with Roman citizens. Regular provincial
government existed. Its circumstance was entirely different from
that of the three areas in the east which had never become part
of the Roman domain. See also 7.3

6.8 *rege Roxolanorum*   See 6.6

6.8 *imminutis stipendiis*   As part of his settlement with Decebalus during his Dacian War, Domitian had agreed to pay a subsidy.
Trajan subsidized the Roxolani as well; reduction in the amount
occurred later, perhaps toward the end of Trajan's reign after
Dacia had become a province. It was this problem which Hadrian
now settled. See 6.6

7.1 *Nigrini*   C. Avidius Nigrinus may be the Nigrinus whom Pliny
praises for activity as *tribunus plebis* in 105 and for oratorical
distinction. If so, this is the only office of which there is
record prior to his suffect consulate in 110. He was subsequently
imperial legate in Achaea and, after that, legate of Dacia, with
his tenure perhaps commencing in 113/14 and lasting until 116/17.
We do not know whether Trajan or Hadrian relieved him. He was
succeeded by C. Julius Quadratus Bassus, who fell in battle the
following year.

His home was Faventia, in Gallia Cisalpina. He was clearly
on good terms with Hadrian, if we may credit the statement that

Commentary 71

he had intended Nigrinus to succeed him. Why, so soon after his own accession, would Hadrian begin to think of a successor for himself? The author's discussion of Hadrian's thoughts for succession come in chap. 23, dealing with the year 136. Therefore the clause, *cum etiam successorem Hadrianus sibimet destinasset*, should perhaps be excised. See 23.10

7.1 *sacrificanti*  Dio LXIX 2.5 speaks of conspiracy during a hunt. Perhaps the two can be reconciled by thinking of a sacrifice in connection with a hunt. This combination appears in the Hadrianic medallions on the Arch of Constantine (see 2.1).

7.1 *Lusio*  See 5.8

7.2 *Palma*  See 4.3

7.2 *Celsus*  See 4.3

7.2 *Nigrinus*  See 7.1

7.2 *Lusius*  See 5.8

7.2 *in vita sua*  See 1.1

7.3 *quattuor consulares*  The "affair of the four consulars" cast a pall over Hadrian's reign which he was never able completely to remove. His relations with the senatorial order were poisoned thereby, and his subsequent oath, that he would not put a senator to death without trial by his peers, had a hollow ring (7.4). Whether he indeed was opposed to their deaths, as he claimed (*invito Hadriano*, 7.2) will never be known; that the senate on its own would authorize the elimination of four of its most distinguished members, two of whom had reached second consulates, appears equally unlikely. Perhaps it was Attianus who was responsible for swaying the senate and having the death penalty applied; he may have thought that thereby he was aiding in the consolidation of Hadrian's nascent principate, by the elimination of potential rivals. An actual conspiracy probably never existed; the four seem to have been linked only because, as Dio LXIX 2.5 said, "they had great influence and enjoyed wealth and fame."

There is a suggestive parallel between this event and the beginning of the reign of Tiberius, with the murder of Agrippa Postumus, *primum facinus novi principatus*, which occurred, Tiberius said, without his knowledge (Tac. *Ann*. I 6).

**7.3** *Romam venit* A doublet, as it appears, with 5.10. This is the proper entry chronologically.

**7.3** *Dacia* See 6.7

**7.3** *Turboni* See 4.2

**7.3** *titulo Aegyptiacae praefecturae* See 4.2 and 6.7

**7.3** *congiarium* See 5.7

**7.4** *iuravit* Was this oath sworn by Hadrian on his own initiative, to win favor, or did it have a standing in law? It appears to be the latter, for there is evidence that almost all emperors subsequent to Augustus swore thus. Not that it prevented the bad emperors from doing away with their enemies; those rulers who did not require such an oath adhered to its limitations. It may somehow have been linked with the decree of the senate whereby it granted the new emperor all the powers that his predecessors had had (the *lex de imperio Vespasiani* is the only such that survives). Septimius Severus went even further (*S* 7.5): *fieri etiam senatus consultum coegit, ne liceret imperatori inconsulto senatu occidere senatorem.* See A. R. Birley (1).

**7.5** *statum cursum fiscalem* Our author here, as elsewhere, varies the customary terminology. He is referring to the *cursus publicus*, the imperial post established on an empire-wide basis by Augustus (Suet. *Aug.* 49.3). Responsibility for maintenance of the post stations and the horses rested with the local communities throughout the empire, and this burden grew heavier as time passed. Nerva freed Italy from further responsibility; an imperial office called, at first, the *a vehiculis*, and later the *praefectus vehiculorum*, existed at least as early as Vespasian's reign. Hadrian extended Nerva's dispensation to the provinces, thereby freeing local magistrates from this oppressive obligation, and taking the expense as a charge on the *fiscus*. In spite of that, the *cursus publicus* continued to be a cause of complaint throughout the provinces in subsequent centuries.

In *AP* 12.3, the author speaks of the *vehicularium cursum* and in *S* 14.2 of the *vehicularium munus*.

**7.6** *infinitam pecuniam . . . incensis* One need not believe that Hadrian's action in destroying the records of uncollected and uncollectable taxes was totally lacking in altruism and that its only purpose was to mitigate his unpopularity stemming from the

elimination of the four consulars. How widely the great mass of
people was affected by such events at the highest level of government is, of course, unknown, but they were probably much more concerned with their own--often financially insecure--existences.
The importance that Hadrian attached to this act is underscored
by its representation on one of the reliefs known as the
"Anaglypha Traiani," with the other representing his actions concerning the alimentary system (see 7.8). Dio LXIX 8.1$^2$ records
that he cancelled debts owed to both the *fiscus* and the *aerarium*.
An inscription found in the Forum of Trajan, dedicated to Hadrian
by the senate and the Roman people in 118, notes the occasion:
*qui primus omnium principum et solus remittendo sestertium novies
milies centena milia n. debitum fiscis non praesentes tantum
cives suos sed et posteros eorum praestitit hac liberalitate
securos* (Smallwood 64 [a]). Sesterii announce the same event and
the amount, which was enormous--900,000,000 sesterces (*BMC* III
417-8, nos. 1206-10; for an example, Smallwood 64 [b]). Dio
also reports that Hadrian fixed a period of fifteen years within
which this remission was to have effect. Does this mean that his
own action covered only debts accruing after 103 (not likely, for
that would have kept still older debts on the books) or that he
established a comparable review of owed revenues, and remission,
every fifteen years, commencing from 118? Yet the only later
instance of anything comparable occurred under Marcus in 178.
Dio's meaning must remain unclear.

The "Anaglypha Traiani" evidently have buildings of the
southern segment of the Roman forum for their background, yet the
literary evidence, and that stemming from the find spot of the
inscription, speak of the Forum of Trajan. The two circumstances
are irreconcilable, unless one has recourse to artistic license.
For discussions of the reliefs and their historical problems, see
Lugli 160-4, Nash 176-7, and above all, with large photographs,
Hammond (1).

7.6 *ex reliquis* "from arrears"

7.7 *damnatorum bona* Confiscation of property followed a wide
range of crimes. The author is in error here, on Hadrian's refusal to allow such property to come to the *fiscus*, with assignment instead to the public treasury. A rescript (*Dig.* XLVIII
8.4.2) states: *eorumque bona merito fisco meo vindicari debere*.
The possessive adjective must be decisive.

7.8 *alimenta* The *alimenta* were an organized system of charity for the upkeep of poor and orphaned children, with support from both the state and private individuals. It appears that Nerva was the first emperor to concern himself with this problem, although it was Trajan who gave the program enormous impetus, which later emperors, particularly Hadrian, continued and expanded. It grew in two stages, the first enrolling poor children among those entitled to free grain in Rome, the second setting up a system of loans to farmers throughout Italy. These farmers put up a substantial part of their land as security, paid the interest to the governing body of their local community, and this interest supported the local children. The farmers were thereby able to improve their own positions and the productivity of Italian agriculture with money for the use of which they paid interest, but they would never repay the principal. The money thus proved to be a government endowment, to use modern terminology.

Hadrian increased the ages up to which children could receive *alimenta*, according to Ulpian (*Dig.* XXXIV 1.14.1): *Certe si usque ad pubertatem alimenta relinquantur, si quis exemplum alimentorum, quae dudum pueris et puellis dabantur, velit sequi, sciat Hadrianum contituisse, ut pueri usque ad decimum octavum, puellae usque ad quartum decimum annum alantur.* Hadrian's concern with the *alimenta* appears to be the subject of the second relief of the "Anaglypha Traiani" (see 7.6). For the alimentary system in general, see Bourne, Duncan-Jones, Garnsey, and Hands.

7.9 *senatoribus . . . patrimonium* Dio LXIX 5.1 reports similar generosity for equites as well. Since Augustus, the census for a senator was 1,000,000 sesterces, for a knight 400,000. This is a difficult sentence; if *modo* does indeed belong here, it will have to mean something like "measure" or "limit," surely in the sense of *numero*. Or is it an ablative depending upon *explevit*; do the words *senatoriae professionis* go with *modo* or, with greater difficulty, with the verb?

Nor is the *ut* clause any clearer. Does *suae* refer to Hadrian or to the senators? Does *dimensum* follow *diem*, or is it the object of the verb? Did Hadrian make one gift to each of the individuals, or was the assistance repeated, perhaps annually, on a particular day (*sine dilatione*)? The confusion is underscored by two quite different English translations: "to many, indeed, he paid punctually on the date the amount allotted for their living" (Magie) and "in such a way that he paid out to many without deferment until the term of their life was measured out" (Birley). Hohl's German rendition is again different: "wobei er in sehr vielen Fällen den zugemessenen Betrag auf Lebenszeit ohne Aufschub gewährte."

The question seems insoluble. We do not know from other sources whether Hadrian preferred to make a single large grant to individuals, to enable them to meet the standards of their order, or smaller annual grants, which were expected to be sent. There is precedent in the earlier empire for both; the phrase *sine dilatione* suggests the latter practice. *Dimensum* will refer to the amount agreed upon, and the *suae* probably refers to the individuals: he paid them what they anticipated annually, on a particular day, and did not fail his obligation.

Centerwell interprets *in diem vitae suae dimensum* as equivalent to *in omnem vitam*, and suggests that Hadrian gave at once a sum of money sufficiently large for the recipients to be able to live for the rest of their lives from the interest which accrued from that capital.

7.10 *ad honores explendos* To enable men to reach the minimum census required for public office (see 7.9), the emperor gave gifts of money.

7.11 *feminas* No external evidence exists to support this claim. If accurate, it is a remarkable innovation, for women were not normally given special assistance, although girls did receive benefit from the *alimenta* (see 7.8).

7.12 *gladiatorium munus* The year is 126. Hadrian was quite modest in his presentations, compared with several of his predecessors. The Colosseum was inaugurated in 80 by Titus with one hundred days of gladiatorial fighting, beast hunts, and other extravaganzas. Trajan, according to Dio LXVIII 15.1, celebrated the conquest of Dacia with 123 days of spectacles in 107, in which ten thousand gladiators fought and eleven thousand animals, both wild and tame, were killed.

8 The whole of this chapter displays respect for the senate, to a greater degree than elsewhere in the Life. Whether this fact can be used to support a view of a particular *Tendenz* is doubtful, although it does seem to fit well with the enhanced position of the Roman senate in the early 390s.

8.1 *contubernium* What does the word mean here? Does it suggest a close personal relationship with the leading men of the senate, whose friendship would gain him support among their order and whose careers he advanced? Or does the author refer to Hadrian's selection of men to participate in his *consilium*, which advised him on political and legal matters? The latter appears more likely, and the use of the word *maiestas* suggests something more formal than mere friendship. If this is what is meant, *contubernium* is used in this context uniquely; nowhere else is it the equivalent of *consilium*. See 8.9 and 18.1, supported by Dio LXIX 7.1, but 9.6 lends credence to the former interpretation.

8.2 *ludos circenses* Games marked by chariot races were celebrated, during the empire, on important anniversaries of the princeps' life and career. There could thus be a substantial number of days each year when no public business could be carried on, and the expense to the public treasury was enormous. Hadrian eliminated almost all those in his honor, according to this statement.

8.3 *rem publicam* What did this concept entail, in a work of the late empire, which long since had lost all resemblance to the Augustan principate, much less the "old republic"? Hadrian's claim links him with Augustus, and thus with the *res publica restituta*, even though it was so different from the form of government which had been dominated by the senate. However, the purpose of government remained the same, the well-being of the *populus*. The contrast is with *regnum*, under which the ruler, concerned primarily with his own position, treats the state as a *res propria*. There are very few statements in the HA of a political-philosophical nature; this must rank as one of the most important. See Béranger (1).

8.4 *tertio consules* Grossly exaggerated. The number of men who reached a third consulate in the early principate is very small, eleven surely known, with one more possible. This was the highest honor that a senator could attain. No *privatus* ever reached a fourth consulate; such eminence was reserved for emperors and members of the ruling family. Forty-nine men gained an iterated consulate, in the period from Augustus through Hadrian; the list is subject to reduction by one. Leaving out of consideration the possibility of prior designation late in one emperor's reign for office which will occur under his successor, the figures are as follows: third consulates, under Augustus 1, Claudius 1, Vespasian 1, Domitian 2 (or 3), Nerva 1, Trajan 3, Hadrian 2; second consulates, under Augustus 2, Gaius 1, Claudius 5, Nero 1, the year of chaos 2, Vespasian 8, Titus 1, Domitian 7

Commentary                                                              77

(or 6), Nerva 1, Trajan 15, Hadrian 6. Trajan himself held six
consulates, Hadrian only three; this difference may be at play
in the feelings of the two emperors about the importance of
iteration in the highest magistracy. Trajan had numerous marshals whose service in war demanded recognition, and many of
them received a second consulate not long after their first.
For full details, see the list in App. V.

8.5 *tertium consulatum* The year is 119, when, unlike the previous year, he was in Rome in January. This passage is the only
source for his resignation from the consulate after four months.
But the practice was common; rarely in the principate did the
*consules ordinarii* hold office for the entire year. We can
certainly accept the statement that Hadrian was much involved in
judicial activities during these four months. Must we assume,
however, that he was unconcerned with that important branch of an
emperor's function when he was not consul? Surely not; how
extensive Hadrian's interest was in the pronouncement of law can
be discerned from a glance at the collection of Hänel 85-101.

   Hadrian never again held a consulate. Trajan had had six,
and the Flavians had dominated the consular fasti almost without
interruption. We can only guess why he was content with so few.

8.6 *senatui legitimo* To reduce the burden of senate attendance
upon its members, Augustus had decreed that the senate should
meet regularly only twice a month, on the Kalends and Ides
(Suet. *Aug.* 35.3). Such a session of the senate was known as a
*senatus legitimus*. But a late calendar informs us that the first
meeting of the month was on the third day in February, March,
June, August, October, and December, and the second meeting also
occurred on the day before the Ides or two days after.

   A special called meeting of the senate was a *senatus
indictus*.

8.7 *fastigium* "rank," "dignity," "prestige"

8.7 *difficile faciens senatores* This is untrue. As were his
predecessors, Hadrian was compelled to adlect fresh blood into
the senate. The almost complete disappearance of patrician
families of republican ancestry required the ennobling of plebe-
ian families, since numbers of religious posts could be filled
only by patricians. So Agricola had been honored: *divus
Vespasianus inter patricios adscivit* (Tac. *Agr.* 9.1).

Continual recruitment to the senate meant that men of lower social status were increasingly chosen, as well as men from the provinces. The first great influx of senators from the east came under Trajan, surprisingly, not Hadrian.

Hadrian does not represent a reaction in the steady pattern of change. New men had to be chosen, either for election to office or adlection, and the emperor's choice was paramount. He could attempt to control quality, not quantity. See Hammond (2).

8.7 *Attianum* See 1.4 and 15.2

8.8 *senatorem* Such a statement, on the occasion of the elevation of Attianus from the highest post in the equestrian cursus to membership in the senate, albeit with consular standing, was excellent public relations for Hadrian in his association with the senate. The execution of the four conslulars early in his reign had made that relationship difficult. See the following note.

8.8 *equites Romanos* One of the prerogatives that the senate jealously guarded was the right for a member of the body to be tried by his peers. An emperor who did not recognize this privilege forfeited good relations with the senate. Since the *senatorius ordo* was the "first estate" of Rome and the *equester ordo* the "second," an equestrian was an inappropriate judge of a senator.

8.9 *consilium* See 8.1 and 18.1

8.9 *sententiam* Evidently, when the emperor heard cases, members of his *consilium* were present to assist him in deliberation. When both sides in the litigation had had their say, the emperor consulted members of the *consilium*, took their advice into account, and then immediately himself delivered his verdict. See Millar 228-40.

8.10 *exsecratus est* The names of those whom he disapproved are nowhere on record. We may assume that Tiberius, Gaius, Nero, and Domitian were included on his list, if, indeed, they did not constitute it in its entirety.

8.11 *Serviano* See 2.6 and 15.8

8.11 *ne esset secundae sententiae* The consul whose name appeared first at the beginning of each year was considered the senior consul and held the *fasces* for the month of January. During the late republic, the man elected first had that honor, although he might for some reason, including age, resign it to his colleague. Augustus changed that practice, in his *Lex de maritandis ordinibus* (18 B.C.); in the words of Gellius (II 15.4-8): *Sicuti capite VII legis Iuliae priori ex consulibus fasces sumendi potestas fit, non qui pluris annos natus est, sed qui pluris liberos quam collega aut in sua potestate habet aut bello amisit. Sed si par utrique numerus liberorum est, maritus aut qui in numero maritorum est praefertur; si vero ambo et mariti et patres totidem liberorum sunt, tum ille pristinus honos instauratur et qui maior natu est prior fasces sumit. . . . Solitos tamen audio, qui lege potiores essent, fasces primi mensis collegis concedere aut longe aetate prioribus aut nobilioribus multo aut secundum consulatum ineuntibus.*

In the imperial *fasti*, however, the emperor's name always stands before his colleague's. Servianus was senior to Hadrian on several counts: age by some thirty years, a second consulship before Hadrian's first, and father of at least one child, while Hadrian had none (see 15.8). Hadrian chose, therefore, not to challenge a law of Augustus on precedence, or a tradition that went back to the beginning of the republic, by holding the consulate with a colleague so senior, and thereby putting himself and his office in the shade. See Taylor and Broughton.

9.1 *multas provincias* Excessive; there were only three, those beyond the Euphrates. See 5.3

9.1 *theatrum* No other evidence exists for the existence of this theatre. If the author is correct in his statement, the building likely stood in the general area of the Campus Martius to which Hadrian devoted so much attention, with the complex of buildings particularly linked with Agrippa's name (see 19.10).

9.2 *simulabat simulare* = to pretend that which is not; *dissimulare* = to conceal that which is. One wonders when Trajan would have given Hadrian such secret instructions, if indeed he had not until the last, if even then, designated him his successor. There is a parallel here with the actions of Marcus Antonius after the murder of Caesar; the consul claimed support from Caesar's papers for a great variety of policies.

9.3 *Attiani* See 1.4 and 15.2

9.3 *quattuor consularium* See 7.3

9.4 *successorem* There was no fixed term for the praetorian prefects. In periods of stress, they could be removed after the briefest service; under Commodus, they changed *per horas ac dies* (*C* 6.6). Conversely, Sejanus served Tiberius for sixteen years, and under Antoninus Pius M. Gavius Maximus reached twenty years (*AP* 8.7). Dio, in the speech which he puts in the mouth of Maecenas (LII 24), urges that the praetorian prefects be appointed for life.

This passage is the only source for the idea that the prefect had the right to remain in office until he asked to be relieved. That does not seem likely, but, if it is, Hadrian evidently made Attianus' position so uncomfortable that he welcomed the opportunity to resign; Similis probably took the hint and submitted his resignation at the same time.

9.4 *Turbonem* See 4.2

9.5 *Simili* Much less is known of the career of Ser. Sulpicius Similis than of Turbo's, with Dio (LXIX 19) again useful. He rose from the ranks, having been a *primipilus*, to the *praefectura annonae*, to the prefecture of Egypt (107-12), and finally to the prefecture of the praetorian guard. His retirement from the last post came in 119. Dio (LXIX 19) charmingly reports that "he spent the rest of his life, seven years, quietly in the country, and upon his tomb he caused this inscription to be placed: 'Here lies Similis, who existed so-and-so many years, and lived seven.'"

9.5 *Septicium Clarum* His political career prior to his appointment as praetorian prefect is unknown, but he clearly was an important figure in literary circles. Pliny the Younger dedicated his collection of letters (either all or the first three books alone, it is not certain) to him: *Frequenter hortatus es ut epistulas, si quas paulo curatius scripsissem, colligerem publicaremque.* He is also the addressee of I 15, VII 28, and VIII 1; none of these is of any particular moment, and one wonders at the substantial gap in the correspondence between them from book I to book VII. He is spoken of in II 9.4 as *quo nihil verius nihil simplicius nihil candidius nihil fidelius novi*. Such a description of his character makes it all the more difficult to understand the cause of his discharge from the command of the praetorians as alleged in 11.3, excessive familiarity with the empress.

Suetonius dedicated his *De Vita Caesarum* to Septicius
Clarus while he was praetorian prefect. Since Turbo is now known
to have been in Pannonia inferior in 123, he cannot have been
Septicius' colleague when the latter and Suetonius were disgraced,
if we accept 122 as the most probable year for this occurrence.
Perhaps Septicius preceded Turbo in office.

9.6 *summotis . . . quibus debebat imperium*  Attianus had been
his tutor (see 1.4) and had been with Trajan during the Parthian
War, being one of those who escorted the ashes of the deceased
to Rome (see 5.9). Similis had been in Rome, and must have played
a role in gaining support for the new emperor in the capital.
Hadrian evidently felt more comfortable with men in this important position who owed him their advancement, rather than with
those who could suggest, by their continuance in office, that
he was in their debt.

9.6 *Campaniam*  Campania possessed one of the two chief harbors
of Italy, Puteoli, Naples (see 19.1), and the remaining attrac-
tions of that lovely bay. His generosity to the various cities
and towns may be inferred from Dio LXIX 5.3: "giving to some a
water supply, to others harbours, food, public works, money and
various honours, differing with the different cities."

9.6 *optimum quemque*  See 8.1

9.7 *frequentavit*  His attendance upon the consuls and praetors
in the performance of their duties was a mark of respect for the
senate, a subject which fills much of chapter 8. This item
would more suitably have appeared there. See also Dio LXIX 7.1.

9.7 *interfuit*  All these aspects of his accustomed behavior
showed his *civilitas*. He did not permit his position to inter-
fere with normal social intercourse. See 17.5 and 20.1

9.8 *ad privati hominis modum*  Extravagance was not part of his
nature. He was simple in his way of life and wished others to be
so as well. See 20.1 and 22.5

9.9 *socrui suae honores praecipuos*  The most significant honor
granted Matidia was deification; she became a *diva* who was worshipped on a public holiday. She was among the twenty *divi* and
*divae* listed in the *feriale Duranum* of approximately a century
later. Marciana, her mother, had also been deified, and Plotina,
Trajan's widow, was surely given the same honor a few years later.

It was Plotina, after all, through whose agency many thought that Hadrian had gained the succession. These three ladies were the first to gain status that can be called permanent in the list of state *divi*. The reason, clearly, was to strengthen Hadrian's own position against those who doubted that he had been Trajan's choice; there were those who thought of him as some had thought of Tiberius: *per uxorium ambitum et senili adoptione inrepsisse* (Tac. *Ann.* I 7.7).

Marciana died August 29, 112; when she was declared *diva*, Matidia was declared *Augusta* (Smallwood 22). When Matidia died in late 119, she was also enrolled among the *divae* and received a splendid funeral *laudatio*, in the old republican tradition, from the emperor (Smallwood 114). Her funeral must indeed have been a splendid occasion, an opportunity for Hadrian to give public display to his relationship with Trajan.

10.1 *variis liberalitatibus* See 9.6

10.2-10.8 This long disquisition on Hadrian's military abilities, practices, and goals appears to have been imposed upon a basic narrative of his travels. The German armies were the first that he visited on this first great tour of empire, and the point chosen by the author for this information is not inappropriate. Nonetheless, it does break the flow of the narrative. Dio (LXIX 9) offers much the same information.

10.2 *militem . . . exercuit* The clearest evidence for the strenuous nature of these maneuvers comes from his review of the army at Lambaesis in the summer of 128 (Smallwood 328). But confirmation of the intensity and variety of these "war games" comes from a tombstone found along the Danube, inscribed with the record of a remarkable swimmer and marksman (Smallwood 336):

*Ille ego Pannoniis quondam notissimus oris*
*inter mille viros fortis primusq. Batavos,*
*Hadriano potui qui iudice vasta profundi*
*aequora Danuvii cunctis transnare sub armis,*
*emissumq. arcu dum pendet in aera telum*
*ac redit ex alia fixi fregique sagitta,*
*quem neque Romanus potuit nec barbarus unquam*
*non iaculo miles, non arcu vincere Parthus,*
*hic situs, hic memori saxo mea facta sacravi.*
*Viderit anne aliquis post me mea facta sequ[a]tur.*
*Exemplo mihi sum primus qui talia gessi.*

How many others performed their exploits *Hadriano iudice*?

Although Hadrian was *pacisque magis quam belli cupidus*, wars were fought during his principate, particularly at its beginning (see 5.2), the most significant and terrible of which was the war against the Jews in his last years. His concern for the army and its readiness to fight caused Fronto (*Princ. Hist.* 10; Haines II 206) to say of him: *(exercitus) ducem neminem umquam post eiusmodi vidit*.

10.2 *manipula* The maniple was the second smallest unit of the legion, in the organization which went back to the early days of the republic. During the early principate, two centuries of eighty men each constituted a maniple; six centuries composed a cohort, and ten cohorts a legion, with the first cohort consisting of five double centuries, a total of 800 men. Thus the use of the word *manipula* here by our author smacks of anachronism, not only for his own time but for Hadrian's, since the maniple had no tactical significance.

10.2 *magistrans* According to Festus (pp. 113, 138 Lindsay), this word is the equivalent of *regere*, *temperare*, and *moderari*.

10.2 *cibis castrensibus* The most important item of the military diet is omitted, *frumentum*, which is our wheat. Vegetables and cheese, along with wine and vinegar, were also basics, and meat was eaten more extensively as years passed; in the late republic and early empire, meat was considered only emergency rations. See Davies (2).

10.2 *Scipionis Aemiliani et Metelli* For the precedents of Scipio in the Numantine War (134-33) and Metellus Numidicus in the war against Jugurtha (109-08), see, respectively, among other sources, Appian *Iber.* 84ff. and Sall. *Jug.* 44-45. Their examples went far beyond the eating of regular soldier's food, as this sentence suggests, but extended to the entire scope of winning over a demoralized army now lacking discipline.

10.2 *multos praemiis, nonnullos honoribus* The random nature of independent evidence makes it impossible to determine whether this statement is accurate; indeed, one cannot tell what precise sense *multos* and *nonnullos* bear. An example of military honors is offered by the career of C. Nummius Constans, *primipilus* of legio II Traiana (Smallwood 311): *donis donato ab imp. Traiano torquibus armillis phaleris ob bellum Parthicum item ab imp. Hadriano corona aurea torquibus armillis phaleris ob bellum Iudeicum*.

10.3 *labantem disciplinam* This is an astonishing statement, for it condemns Trajan as well as other emperors who clearly should be acquitted of a charge of *incuria*. Tiberius and Vespasian, themselves skillful commanders of long experience in the field, certainly maintained the quality of training which they knew was essential. Trajan's enormous prestige and recognition as *optimus princeps* depended in large part upon his reputation as a general and his success in the Dacian wars; his armies were first-class fighting instruments. One wonders what the author of these biographies said about Trajan's concern for military discipline (assuming, as I do, that the collection included his biography), since Pliny (*Ep*. X 29) speaks of him as *conditorem disciplinae militaris firmatoremque*. But one of the general themes of Roman historiography in the late republic and early empire is that almost every general and emperor must begin anew; his predecessors have allowed the armies to sink into desuetude. So Metellus in Africa, Marius in Gaul, Corbulo in Syria, Cerialis in Britain, Agricola too as legionary commander. Hadrian's concern for discipline is supported independently by his allocutions to the troops at Lambaesis (Smallwood 328); in this he was following in Trajan's footsteps, not pursuing a different policy. After Augustus, Hadrian had the most responsibility for the patterns of administration and discipline of the imperial army.

10.3 *officiis et inpendiis* It had been common practice for soldiers to buy release from unpleasant duties. This was one of the complaints voiced by the soldiers in the Pannonian revolt at the beginning of Tiberius' reign: *denis in diem assibus animam et corpus aestimari; hinc vestem arma tentoria, hinc saevitiam centurionum et vacationes munerum redimi* (Tac. *Ann*. I 17.4). Otho gained favor by making the purchase of these exemptions a levy upon the *fiscus*, a move which Tacitus approved (*Hist*. I 46. 4): *fiscum suum vacationes annuas exsoluturum promisit, rem haud dubie utilem et a bonis postea principibus perpetuitate disciplinae firmatam.*

Nonetheless, in spite of Otho's action and its continuance by some of his successors, abuses clearly were not eliminated. Hadrian's stricter discipline prevented *vacationes* and thereby saved himself and the troops money. If tasks had to be routinely done, no one had cause for complaint. See 10.7

10.4 *commendaret* Hadrian's choice of officers on the basis of merit rather than popularity had a precedent in Agricola's action

(*Agr.* 19.2): *non studiis privatis nec ex commendatione aut precibus centurionem militesve adscire, sed optimum quemque fidissimum putare.* See 10.6

**10.4** *triclinia* Officers' quarters in permanent stone fortresses must have gradually taken on the appearance of private and civilian mansions, with many of the appointments of comfort itemized here. The *praetorium*, the residence of the commanding officer of the unit, frequently with bath attached, could rival luxurious villas. Hadrian evidently forbade all that, and restored the appearance of the military camp to the simplicity and regularity that it had developed.

**10.6** *hospitiis* "in their own quarters" Or can we take *hospitia* here in the sense of *valetudinarium*, "hospital," a meaning not uncommon in mediaeval Latin.

The Roman army had no medical services before Hellenistic times, but during the empire treatment of the sick and wounded improved enormously, as *valetudinaria* became an integral part of encampments and sanitary measures were improved. Inscriptions speak of soldiers who were known as *medicus ordinarius, medicus cohortis,* or *medicus legionis,* soldiers who became experienced in medicine, not physicians who served with the armies.

In the permanent stone legionary fortress, the hospital was normally part of the central cluster of buildings, along with the headquarters building (*principia*), the general's residence(*praetorium*), and the granaries (*horrea*). See Scarborough 66-75.

**10.6** *locum castris caperet* This is a commonplace of great generals. One need only instance Vespasian (Tac. *Hist.* II 5.1, *locum castris capere*) and Agricola (*Agr.* 20.2, *loca castris ipse capere*).

**10.6** *vitem* The *vitis* was symbolic of the centurion's rank, and signified his power to maintain discipline. The fate of the centurion Lucilius, during the revolt of the legions in Pannonia in 14 A.D., is instructive (Tac. *Ann.* I 23.3): *et centurio Lucilius interficitur, cui militaribus facetiis vocabulum 'Cedo alteram' indiderant quia fracta vite in tergo militis alteram clara voce ac rursus aliam poscebat.* A centurion could rise through the ranks to become a *primipilus*, if he were good enough, or he could be directly appointed by the emperor. The *primipili* were invariably men of mature years, from the forties on into the sixties. See Watson 86ff.

10.6 *tribunum* During the early principate, the tribunes were customarily appointed by the emperor. They varied in age, but could be as young as eighteen. They were assigned posts by the *legatus legionis*; their duties were chiefly administrative, but they might be put in command of military units. Equestrian tribunes also commanded auxiliary units, both cavalry and infantry. When the emperor chose individuals for this post, he was making a judgment of quality and ability without much previous opportunity to have tested them. This was an important stage in both the senatorial and equestrian cursus for those who looked forward to a career in the emperor's service.

Hadrian's practice of choosing men of sufficient maturity is recalled by the author in *Pr* 4.3: *Valerianus Augustus Mulvio Gallicano praef. praet. mireris fortassis, quod inberbem tribunum fecerim contra sententiam divi Hadriani.*

Apropos both for this note and the one preceding is a quotation from Florus, regarding the emperor's patronage (*Vergilius Orator an Poeta* 3.5): *nempe si mihi maximus imperator vitem id est centum homines regendos tradidisset, non mediocris honor habitus mihi videretur; cedo si praefecturam, si tribunatum: nempe idem honos, nisi quod merces amplior.*

10.8 *aetatibus* A recruit might be as young as eighteen. At the beginning of the empire, there was a differentiation between legions and *auxilia* in length of service, twenty years total for the former and twenty-five for the latter. But men were often held on service after the expiration of their term. This was one of the chief complaints voiced in the mutiny of the Pannonian legions at the beginning of Tiberius' principate (Tac. *Ann.* I 17.2): *satis per tot annos ignavia peccatum, quod tricena aut quadragena stipendia senes et plerique truncato ex vulneribus corpore tolerent.* By the second century, the routine period of service was twenty-five years, for legionary and auxiliary alike.

10.8 *noti essent* His memory must have been quite remarkable to keep so many names and faces straight, particularly with the passage of years. See the engaging anecdote about a veteran in 17.6, and 20.10.

10.8 *numerus* Each military unit had a standard number of personnel, but only rarely would all men have been on duty

simultaneously and in the same place. Some would be on sick
call, some on leave, some serving in *vexillationes* elsewhere,
some off on fatigue duty, some detached for other purposes. And,
indeed, units were frequently understrength. Every unit had to
know, daily, how many men were assigned to it and what the status
of each was, and daily registers were kept by the headquarters
staff. Annual reports of personnel status were also made; for
such an example, dating to the early years of Trajan, known as
"Hunt's *Pridianum*", see Fink.

11.1 *condita militaria* "military stores" It was essential that
each military establishment, from the smallest to the legionary
fortress, have sufficient reserve to withstand a lengthy siege.
Agricola had seen to this (Tac. *Agr.* 22.2): *nam adversus moras
obsidionis annuis copiis firmabantur.* We do not know whether
grain was stored loose in bins or in barrels, nor how much space
the estimated annual ration of a soldier occupied, nor where
other items such as meat, oil, and wine were stored. But it
appears that granaries were large enough to hold two years'
supply from the time of the most recent harvest.

11.1 *reditus provinciales* These refer not to the tributes that
went into the *fiscus* or *aerarium* at Rome, but to the contributions
in kind that were made by the provincials to the military establishment, consisting of such things as foodstuffs, metals, and
leather. Those which were short Hadrian undertook to make good
from other sources, so that every military unit and post had
precisely the facilities, equipment, and supplies that the table
of organization indicated that it should have.

11.2 *regio more* "by the example which he, the emperor, set"
The adjective *regius* is not customarily applied to good emperors
in the early principate; its use here is characteristic of a
late date. Or, perhaps, "in regal fashion."

11.2 *Brittaniam* The province mentioned before Britain is Germany, but he did not travel directly between the two. He made
an inspection also of the Danube provinces nearest Germany,
Raetia and Noricum, before crossing the Channel.
    Hadrian probably brought A. Platorius Nepos with him to
take over the governorship of Britain (see 4.2). His predeces-
sor was Q. Pompeius Falco, who may well have been responsible
for putting down a serious uprising, probably on the part of
the Brigantes. It was evidently this event which caused Hadrian

to plan the great wall which bears his name, which ran for some eighty Roman miles (as our author states; about seventy-three English miles) from the Tyne on the east to the Solway on the west, reaching from the modern town of Wallsend east of Newcastle to Bowness west of Carlisle, with further defensive installations along the Cumberland coast looking out to the Irish sea.

The purpose of the Wall was to separate those within the empire from those without and to control movement from one side to the other. Its construction exemplified Hadrian's policy of establishing tangible and visible boundaries wherever possible (see 12.6). It is worth noting that this is the only reference to the Wall in ancient literature. The history of Hadrian's Wall, its construction and survival, is long and complex. In general, see Frere.

11.3 *Septicio Claro* See 9.5. Did this occur in Rome or in Britain? Probably the latter, since the affair follows so closely upon mention of Britain and the construction of the Wall, although the author is not known for careful chronological connections. The praetorian prefect and the heads of the imperial bureaucracy customarily accompanied the emperor on his travels. See Millar 90-1.

11.3 *Suetonio Tranquillo* The discovery of an inscription at Hippo Regius in Africa, in 1952, has furnished valuable information on the career of the renowned biographer, C. Suetonius Tranquillus. Born about 70, he spent much of his early manhood as a teacher (*grammaticus*) and became a close friend of Pliny, who gained a military tribunate for him in 101, which, however, Suetonius chose not to take up. While he was in Bithynia, Pliny wrote Trajan requesting the *ius trium liberorum* for Suetonius, which the emperor granted; it may be that Suetonius was serving on Pliny's staff. Trajan adlected Suetonius *inter selectos*, which meant he served as a *iudex*, a post appropriate for a scholar. He then held, successively, the posts *a studiis*, *a bybliothecis*, and *ab epistulis* (here he is called *epistularum magister*), the first two perhaps under Trajan, the last under Hadrian, and it was this from which he was dismissed. The task of the *a studiis* was, perhaps, to assist the emperor in his composition of speeches and letters, the *a bybliothecis* was in charge of the public libraries, and the *ab epistulis* responsible for imperial correspondence. The last post was one of the major ones in the imperial bureaucracy.

Suetonius' dismissal in disgrace probably occurred in 122. We do not know how much longer he lived. Although the first two Lives are the fullest, the later ones also include archival material, and it has been suggested that those from Galba on were composed before those chronologically earlier. But he might well have composed straight on, in chronological order, and been able to work from notes after he no longer had access to the imperial files. See Pflaum (1) #96; Smallwood 281; Bowersock (2).

If, however, the assumption is made that this passage is an intrusion into the basic text and out of chronological order, then Suetonius need not have been dismissed as early as 122 and may have remained in the emperor's favor as late as 128. For this argument, see Crook (2) and Gascou. But it does not seem compelling.

11.3 *multisque aliis* Concerning these nothing is known, if there were any others. See 23.8 for the identical expression, similarly without support.

11.3 *Sabinam uxorem* See 2.10, 23.9

11.4 *curiosus* See 14.11 and 15.2

11.4 *frumentarios* The original charge of the *frumentarii* was the *annona militaris*, responsibility for the army commissary. Later they were used as military messengers and then as the imperial messenger service, an innovation assigned to the reign of Trajan by Victor (13.5-6): *simul noscendis ocius, quae ubique e republica gerebantur, admota media publici cursus. Quod equidem munus satis utile in pestem orbis Romani vertit posteriorum avaritia insolentiaque.* Transition to secret police functions followed easily, and it is clear in this passage that Hadrian used their services in espionage to discover wrongdoing, or suggested impropriety or immorality, not only in his own household but in those of others. See Sinnigen.

11.6 *commeatum* "leave," "permission to travel" A senator could not travel wherever he wished without permission. Augustus had required senators to live in Italy, but had allowed those with property in Sicily to visit it without permission, and Claudius had extended that privilege to those who were landowners in Gallia Narbonensis. The purpose of this prohibition was evidently to keep senators on the job or within relatively easy call for sessions of the senate. Even Pliny the Younger, while in office as *praefectus aerarii Saturni*, requests leave from Trajan to travel in Italy (*Ep.* X 8[24].6): *si mihi ob utraque haec dederis commeatum triginta dierum.*

11.7 *amore . . . adulteriis* This sounds like scandal, for which there is no evidence. The only women with whose names Hadrian is linked were Plotina and his wife Sabina; homosexual relations are suggested in 2.7 and with Antinous (14.5). The source is perhaps Marius Maximus.

11.7 *fidem* See 15.2

12.1 *ob Apidem* Apis was the sacred bull, distinguished by various external marks, which was believed to have come to life in miraculous ways. Herodotus reported at length about the animal and its worship. Other mentions of Apis in the imperial era are under Vespasian (Suet. *Tit.* 5.3) and Julian (Amm. XXII 14.6). Any riot that ensued upon the occasion of his appearance could not have been because of rivalry over where the god would reside; its residence was always in Memphis (Pliny *NH* VIII 185). The participants in this *seditio* were clearly the Egyptians, not the Greek populace of Alexandria.

This report is out of chronological sequence. The uprising probably occurred soon after Hadrian's accession, and was quelled by a letter from the emperor (Dio LXIX 8.1[a]).

12.2 *basilicam apud Nemausum* For this basilica in Nimes, cf. Smallwood 142: *Iovi et Nemaus. T. Flavius Herm. exactor oper. basilicae marmorari et lapidari v(otum) s(olvit).* That must have been a profitable contract. See 2.10

12.3 *aedem Augusti* Augustus waged war against the Cantabri of northwestern Spain during 26 B.C. Becoming ill during the latter part of the campaign, he withdrew to Tarraco to convalesce. He thus grew fond of the city, gave it many honors, and in turn the citizens dedicated an altar to him. After his death, the altar was replaced by a temple of Divus Augustus, in the year 15. It was this that, evidently, had suffered the ravages of time, which Hadrian now, at the expense of the *fiscus*, restored.

12.4 *omnibus . . . consuluit* Hadrian, surprisingly, never visited his *patria* of Italica while emperor (Dio LXIX 10.1). Tarraco, his base for Spain, was the nearest large and important city to the province of Narbonensis, well located in the event a sudden departure was necessary, whether by land or sea. A major, if not the major, purpose of his visit to the Spains was the need for troops; there had been a major reversal in Britain only a few years before and there was still tension in the east, after the suppression of the revolts that had begun late in Trajan's reign and the establishment of the new provincial order with the resignation of three of Trajan's newly-won provinces. Spain had for long been a major source of recruits, although not extensively in the most recent decades; the inhabitants now evidently considered that they deserved freedom from the levy for replacements in existing legions as much as did Italians. New legions continued to be raised in Italy. And they clearly won their case; Hadrian took other measures.

The text has recently been challenged by Syme (5) 145. He proposes *omnibus Hispanis . . . retractantibus, Italicis vehementissime <suscensuit>, ceteris prudenter caute <que> consuluit*. The *Italici* being the citizens of Italica, and not people of Italian origin or rights, whatever they might be, the text still, he claims, makes no sense with a comma after *Italicis*, nor is there "a verb to govern 'Italicis' and stand in the requisite antithesis to 'ceteris . . . consuluit'. . . . Hadrian was 'exceedingly wroth' with the Italicenses, his fellow-townsmen, and with them alone." Granted that a contrast is called for, need we invoke textual corruption? Quite a different sense is produced by alteration of the punctuation: *omnibus Hispanis . . . vocatis dilectumque iocularitier retractantibus Italicis, vehementissime ceteris, . . .* , where the meaning will be that all resisted the levy, the Italici with good humor (surely feeling confident in their relation with the emperor) and the others with vehemence, and that Hadrian responded to both groups with wisdom and restraint. So too Centerwell.

Nierhaus 157ff. similarly disputes Syme, maintaining the text as it is, but he does not insert a comma after *ceteris*. The ablative absolute embraces everything from *omnibus* through *ceteris*. But he argues that the distinction between *Italici* and *ceteri* is not one of provenience, and that the former are not the *Italicenses*. Rather, even though all are citizens and there is no legal distinction between them, the *Italici* refer to those who brought their Roman citizenship with them to Spain many generations ago or obtained it in the early empire, while the others became citizens subsequent to 74, when Vespasian raised the status of native towns to *municipia* of Latin status, whose local magistrates obtained Roman citizenship.

For Hadrian's speech *de Italicensibus*, see 20.7.

12.4 *Marius Maximus*   See 2.10

12.5 *virdiaria*   A garden planted with trees

12.5 *servo in se hospitis*   The word order seems peculiar; *hospitis* should not be separated from *servo* by the prepositional phrase, which is construed with *inruente* and should more directly precede it.

12.5 *in nullo omnino commotus*   See 5.5

12.6 *barbari . . . dividuntur*   The great example of a barrier to keep the barbarians out of Roman territory is, of course, the wall in Britain (11.2). The palisades here described were built in Germany, Dacia, and Africa. This is the only reference to the German *limes* in ancient literature. It ran for some 550 kilometers from Rhine to Danube, jutting eastward to embrace a vast territory between those two rivers. As in Britain, Hadrian established a static frontier. See E. Birley (2).

12.6 *funditus*   "deeply"

12.7 *Germanis regem constituit*   Details of this event are unknown. It probably occurred in late 121, in consequence of his expansion of the *limes*, which caused the Germans on the far side of the Rhine to recognize Rome's superiority and consequently to invite the emperor to settle internal disputes by appointing a king for them. This followed a practice that went back to the days of Augustus, with Roman influence upon internal German politics. This instance evidently illustrates Dio's statement (LXIX 9.6) that Hadrian was invited by barbarians to arbitrate their disputes.

12.7 *motus Maurorum*   Most lists of Hadrian's journeys include a visit to Mauretania in this year (123) in order to crush the uprising there in person. Chowen (3) has argued that this need not be; any victory would be won under the emperor's auspices and thus the senate would decree *supplicationes* in his honor. Two other passages refer to visits to Africa, in the widest geographical sense rather than the narrow political sense of the old province: 13.4 and 22.14. The last passage, reporting the welcome rain that broke a five-year drought on the occasion of his arrival, must refer to the visit recorded in the former, during which he visited not only Africa Proconsularis but also

Commentary                                                          93

Lambaesis in Numidia and Mauretania. Hence Hadrian's only visit
to Africa occurred during his second great journey, in 128. See
5.2

12.7 *supplicationes* During the republic, thanksgivings occurred
in periods of crisis or of great national joy, as after a significant victory over an enemy. The number of days decreed by the
senate for the *supplicatio* varied greatly, and the honor granted
the *triumphator* was commensurate. Caesar's after the victory
over Vercingetorix was for twenty days; the longest recorded is
fifty. Augustus was honored with fifty-five *supplicationes*, for
a total of 890 days. In the empire the *supplicatio* was linked
only with victory or the occurrence of a propitious event in the
imperial family. We do not know how many *supplicationes* Hadrian
received, nor the total of the days celebrated. See Wissowa
423ff.

12.8 *bellum Parthorum* This dispute was perhaps over the king-
ship of Osroene, a Parthian vassal state located in northwestern
Mesopotamia. Evidently, Parthamaspates (see 5.4) had died, and
disagreement developed between Rome and Parthia over a successor.

12.8 *conloquio* For the emperor to appear in person at such a
conference was an innovation. In the first century, he had always been represented by a deputy, as Augustus by Tiberius in 20
B.C., Tiberius by Germanicus, and Nero by Corbulo. The prestige
of the emperor himself was not immediately placed on the line.
The date is 123. See Ziegler 117.

13.1 *Eleusinia sacra exemplo Herculis Philippique* Initiation
into the Eleusinian Mysteries required two stages, at least a
year apart. Though one might assume that the emperor could receive dispensation from this requirement, it does not appear that
this was either asked or given. Hadrian thus became a "mystic"
(μύστης) in 124 or 125, a "seer" (ἐπόπτης) in 128 or 129.
Philip is perhaps mentioned as one of his predecessors in the
rites of initiation because the Macedonian royal house stemmed
from Hercules. Yet it seems very strange that Athens' bitterest
enemy should gain entry into her most sacred rites; nonetheless,
most studies of Hadrian accept the statement. But Oliver (3)
proposes to read *Philopappi* for *Philippi*, invoking the man whose
monument dominated the Hill of the Muses (see Travlos 462-65).
Hadrian's Athenian experiences closely paralleled those of the
older man; "the adoption of Athens by Philopappus and of

Philopappus by Athens set a precedent for Hadrian." But
Philopappus, a private citizen, seems weak precedent for an
emperor.

On Hadrian's religion in general, see Beaujeu and Guarducci.
On the Mysteries, Mylonas 224-85; one of his statements on this
final page is illuminating: "we cannot help but believe that
the Mysteries of Eleusis were not an empty, childish affair devised by shrewd priests to fool the peasant and the ignorant, but
a philosophy of life that possessed substance and meaning and
imparted a modicum of truth to the yearning human soul. That
belief is strengthened when we read in Cicero that Athens has
given nothing to the world more excellent or divine than the
Eleusinian Mysteries." The Cicero reference is *De Leg.* II 14.
36.

Hadrian at the Eleusinian Mysteries is also mentioned by
Hieronymus, *Ad Magnum Oratorem* IV: *Quadratus Apostolorum discipulus, et Atheniensis Pontifex Ecclesiae, nonne Adriano Principi,
Eleusinae sacra invisenti, librum pro nostra religione tradidit?
Et tantae admirationi omnibus fuit, ut persecutionem gravissimam,
illius excellens sedaret ingenium.*

13.1 *multa in Athenienses contulit* Hadrian had enormous impact
on the political and economic life of Athens. He brought about
constitutional change by issuing a new code of law, based upon
the laws of Draco and Solon whenever possible, he changed the
*boule* by reducing the number of its members, he reformed public
finances, established a new tribe bearing his name, *Hadrianis*,
and altered the right of appear. On the establishment of the
Panhellenion, see 13.6. See Follet (2) 107-26, Graindor 73-114,
Day 183-96.

13.1 *pro agonotheta* The ἀγωνοθέτης was the president of the
games. The occasion was the Dionysia of March 125.

13.2 *Achaia* The Roman province of Greece.

13.2 *cultros* Knives were an integral part of the paraphernalia
of such cults as those of Cybele and Dionysus. Their availability in the presence of the emperor, of course, brought fear
of assassination.

13.3  *Aetnam montem*  The great mountain which dominates the northeastern point of the island, the only active volcano in Europe today.  For the ascent, cf. 14.3.

13.3  *Arcus . . . varium*  "many-coloured . . . like a rainbow" (A. Birley)

13.4  *Africam*  See 12.7.  By use of the word *atque* the author ignores Hadrian's presence in Rome and Italy which lasted some two and a half years.

13.4  *multum beneficiorum*  See 9.6

13.5  *tantum terrarum*  This is quite true; the only one of his predecessors who could match him at all was Augustus, who, nonetheless, did not visit as many provinces as he did nor stay away from Italy for as long at a stretch.  For Hadrian's journeys, see 17.8 and App. IV.

13.6  *Iovis Olympii aedem*  This temple, begun in the sixth century B.C., remained unfinished for more than six hundred years and was at last completed, on a monumental scale, by Hadrian. It is one of the few temples in the ancient world measuring more than one hundred meters in length, and the only one in mainland Greece.  Since the only temple of comparable size in Rome and Italy is Hadrian's to Venus and Rome, it would appear that, to Hadrian, grandeur embraced the concept of enormous size.  See Travlos 402-11.  His own statue stood in the temple (Dio LXIX 16.1) and he himself was subsequently entitled Olympius (Smallwood 143, 144).  At Cyzicus he was honored as the thirteenth Olympian, *deus tertius decimus*.  Nonetheless, following the precedent of his worthy predecessors, he refused some of the divine honors offered him by the Achaeans in 126, who style him θειότατος (see Oliver [1]).  Cistophoric tetradrachms with the legend IOVIS OLYMPIUS were issued in his honor in conjunction with his visit to Ephesus in 129 (see Metcalf).

 The chronology of Hadrian's work on the temple appears to be more complex than this passage suggests:  the work began in 124/5, dedication of part of the temple followed in 128/9, and the entire complex was completed in 131/2.

13.6  *aram*  This altar has not survived, nor is its location known.  Hadrian was more concerned with the wide dissemination of the imperial cult as a means of the emotional unification of the empire than any of his predecessors other than Augustus.  As

Zeus Olympios was the chief of the gods, so Hadrianos Olympios
was the foremost among humans; this was his most popular epithet,
far exceeding Panhellenios. He was linked with Zeus by the dedication in his honor of statues at the Olympieium by cities from
all over the Greek world, and close to three hundred altars set
up to Hadrian have thus far been discovered throughout the Greek
world, 94 of them in Athens alone (See Benjamin).

Even though Hadrian did not use the title Panhellenios as
much as Olympios, the former commemorated his establishment of the
Panhellenion, with Athens as its center, in 131/2. He thereby
left no doubt that, to him, Athens had long been the leading
city of the Greek world, intellectually, religiously, and morally.
Along with his constitutional reforms and the establishment of a
new tribe (see 13.1), this was his most significant achievement
in Athens.

13.6 *templa sui nominis* These are temples of the imperial cult
in Asia along with a central shrine in Phaselis, in Lycia, in
which the neighboring cities placed their statues. One should
not think of temples dedicated to him alone; he will always have
been linked with a divinity, as he was represented as Zeus
Olympios.

13.7 *Capadocibus* Cappadocia's importance stemmed largely from
its crucial location in east-central Asia Minor, fronting Armenia.
The Cappadocian dynasty came to an end with its annexation as a
province in 17 A.D.; at first procuratorial, it was joined with
Galatia and Armenia Minor by Vespasian and was governed by a
legate of consular rank. Trajan combined it with Pontus, thereby
giving one consular legate command of the entire land mass north
of Cilicia and Commagene. Flavius Arrianus was governor from 134
to 137.

There had been two legions in Cappadocia when the Parthian
War began, XII Fulminata and XVI Flavia Firma. Under Hadrian
only the former remained, with its fortress at Melitene. The
*servitia* mentioned here will have been the serfs belonging to the
native aristocracy and the temples. Their function, evidently,
was to perform the fatigue duties attendant upon any military
establishment.

13.8 *toparchas* "Toparchs" are governors of districts; τοπαρχία
is one of the equivalents of the Latin *pagus* found in imperial
inscriptions.

13.8 *Osdroe rege Parthorum* Osdroes = Osroes = Chosroes, Trajan's enemy, father of Parthamaspates. Trajan had replaced the father with the son; Hadrian removed the latter and reinstated the former. This trip was in 129. In actuality, the *sella* was not returned, because Osdroes refused Hadrian's invitation. See Ziegler 109.

13.9 *qui venire noluerunt* See 21.13

13.9 *Farasmanis* This king of Iberia, a land just south of the Caucasus, seems to have been the most frustrating of all foreign kings for Hadrian to deal with. He was clearly contemptuous toward the Romans, and Hadrian, perhaps in a fit of pique, replied in kind when given the opportunity (17.12). Pharasmanes was responsible for an invasion by the Alani, a Sarmatian tribe from north of the Caucasus who must have passed with safe conduct through his own lands, of Albania, Media Atropatene, Armenia, and Cappadocia. They were finally repelled by a combination of bribery from Vologaesus of Parthia and their fear of Flavius Arrianus, the governor of Cappadocia. Vologaesus accused Pharasmanes to the Romans, but the outcome of this action is unknown. The date is 136. See Dio LXIX 15.

Surprisingly, Pharasmanes' relations with Antoninus were much more cordial (*AP* 9.6).

13.10 *procuratores et praesides* This statement can hardly be believed. Procurators were officials appointed by the emperor, normally equestrian but occasionally freedmen, who governed minor provinces or were concerned with imperial finances. The word *praeses* is anachronistic in the second century; it is only in the third that it gains popularity, to indicate a provincial governor of equestrian, not senatorial, status.

Provincial administration is one of the aspects of life which made the principate of Augustus welcome to the empire, according to Tac. *Ann.* I 2.2: *neque provinciae illum rerum statum abnuebant, suspecto senatus populique imperio ob certamina potentium et avaritiam magistratuum, invalido legum auxilio, quae vi ambitu, postremo pecunia turbabantur.* But the constant recurrence during the early principate of cases of extortion clearly showed that even a conscientious emperor was incapable of protecting all his subjects constantly. Our author frequently speaks of emperors' concern for provincials, but the words *supplicio* and *severe* are not supported by other evidence. For provincial maladministration, see Brunt.

The implication that Hadrian was responsible for the *accusatores* recalls the earlier charge (11.4) of his use of *frumentarii* as espionage agents.

13.10 *crederetur* Normally intransitive, *credo* is occasionally used personally in the passive.

14.1 *Antiochenses* This sentence assumes a dislike on Hadrian's part for which there is no evidence. He was in Antioch on three different occasions, first during the last two years of the Parthian War, then in 123, and finally in 129. He was responsible for a substantial amount of building in the city and its suburb of Daphne, particularly in connection with the water supply. One would assume that the city would appeal to him, because of its central significance in Greek culture.

The change proposed in the status of Syria was accomplished by Septimius Severus in 195, following his defeat of Pescennius Niger. The province was divided into two, Syria Coele and Syria Phoenice. Our statement that Hadrian had intended this administrative step to humble the Antiochenes is doubtful and probably anachronistic. But the status of Antioch was indeed lessened by the emperor's designation of Tyre, Damascus, and Samosata as metropoleis.

14.2 *Iudaei* The reason given here, the prohibition of circumcision, should probably be considered, indeed, the main cause of the outbreak of war. Secondary was Hadrian's decision to found the city of Aelia Capitolina on the site of Jerusalem, with a temple to Jupiter where the synagogue, destroyed by Titus, had stood. This began in 130, but the war did not break out until 132, so that the chronology of the narrative here is confused, for the date of Hadrian's travels as presented in this chapter is 130 (see App. IV). The period between the foundation and the Bar Kochba revolt should be kept in mind. Dio has the main information (LXIX 12-14). The foundation of the Roman colony has been called Hadrian's "supreme folly" (Barnard). But his aversion to circumcision may have been a still greater folly. The prohibition affected Nabataeans, Samaritans, and Egyptians as well as Jews. It was a sweeping measure, too much so to Antoninus' mind, who permitted the Jews, and only the Jews, to renew the practice (*Dig.* XLVIII 8.11): *Circumcidere Iudaeis filios suos tantum rescripto divi Pii permittitur.* For full discussion, see Smallwood (2) 428-66.

14.3 *monte Casio* Located some twenty miles from Antioch, about a mile in height. Cf. the similar ascent of Mount Aetna, also to see the sunrise (13.3). An epigram that Hadrian composed for a dedication by Trajan to Zeus Casios has survived (*Anth. Pal.* 6,332). Schwartz (2) 247 claims that this climb never occurred but was based upon an exploit of Julian.

14.3 *decidens* The *i* is long; the verb is compounded from *caedo*, not *cado*. The two accusatives are its objects.

14.3 *sacrificanti* This is, of course, Hadrian. The verb *adflavit* implies some injury; was Hadrian knocked unconscious? It seems unlikely that he would have totally escaped when the animal and attendant, in close proximity to him, were mortally struck. For a dream of a similar yet different occurrence, see Dio LXIX 2.1.

14.4 *peragrata Arabia* We know that he visited Gerasa and Petra.

14.4 *Pelusium* Located at the eastern mouth of the Nile, this city was strategic for the defense of Egypt against the east, Arabia and Palestine. He who controlled it and Alexandria controlled access to Egypt; hence Tacitus speaks of the two cities as the *claustra Aegypti* (*Hist.* II 82.3) and the *claustra terrae et maris* (*Ann.* II 59.3).

14.4 *Pompei tumulum* When Pompey was defeated by Caesar at Pharsalus, he fled to Egypt, hoping for refuge. But he was murdered as he came ashore; his head was cut off and sent to Caesar, his body was thrown into the sea. Caesar wept when he beheld the head of his onetime son-in-law and great rival and punished those responsible; a freedman recovered the body and gave it burial under a modest tomb. Statues were later added to make the whole a more impressive monument, but with the passage of time the statues were removed to a temple and the tomb itself obliterated by sand. Hadrian undertook to return the statues to their proper place and restored the monument. Dio (LXIX 11.1) reports that he uttered the following verse:

"Strange lack of tomb for one with shrines o'erwhelmed!"
See Pekáry.

14.5 *Antinoum* The relationship between Hadrian and the handsome Bithynian youth whom he evidently met the year before has been the subject of gossip and debate since antiquity. The author here suggests that Antinous offered himself to save Hadrian's life and that there was a homosexual relationship between them. Tradition also reported that Antinous committed suicide because an oracle had stated that, if he did so, the remaining years of life that he could expect would be transferred to the emperor. There is even the possibility, unsensational as it is, that the childless emperor, whose relationship with his wife was at best cool, looked upon the attractive young man as the son whom he had never had. Whatever the facts were, Hadrian's grief was extravagant, and he caused the youth to be worshipped as a god throughout the empire and cities in his honor were established in numerous places. An Antinoopolis rose along the Nile near the spot where he drowned. The date of his death is October 30, 130. See Dio LXIX 11.2-4; Victor 14.7-9; Clairmont.

14.6  *aliis quod . . . Hadriani*  Suggestion of a homosexual relationship.

14.7  *oracula*  Oracles were one of the means whereby priests and private individuals with special talents were able to forecast the future. But there were also those who played on people's credulity; fraud was involved here, whether the prime responsibility was the emperor's or the natives'. See 2.4

14.8  *poematum et litterarum*  See 14.9, 16.1-4, 25.9-10. Dio LXIX 3.1 tells of his fluency in both languages and his compositions in both of verse and prose.

14.9  *picturae peritissimus*  See 16.10. He himself modelled and painted (Dio LXIX 3.2).

14.9  *versibus*  See 14.3, 16.4, 25.9-10. If indeed there were verses *de suis dilectis*, they have not survived.

14.10  *rei militaris scientissimus*  See the whole of chapter 10.

14.10  *gladiatoria arma*  Credit for the use of gladiatorial weapons and gladiatorial instructors in the training of legionaries is given to P. Rutilius Rufus, cos. 105 B.C. (Valerius Maximus II 3.2). The weapons were heavier than regular military issue and more difficult to manipulate.

14.11  *semper in omnibus varius*  Compare the description in Tertullian, *Apol.*5.7: *omnium curiositatum explorator*, and in the *Epit.* 14.6: *varius multiplex multiformis*. See 11.4

15.1 *non petentes, cum petentibus*  See 2.10 on Plotina, 17.3, and 22.9

15.2 *quidquid insusurrabatur*  See 11.4

15.2 *Attianum*  For his early importance in Hadrian's career, see 1.4. He was with Trajan at the latter's death, probably as praetorian prefect. He may, in that capacity, have been responsible for the elimination of the four consulars, and early urged the removal of other men of rank (5.5 and 9.3). Soon after Hadrian's accession, Attianus lost favor with his former ward; Hadrian may have resented the older man's behavior toward him, he may have felt obligated toward Attianus for support at Trajan's death, we do not know. Desire to kill Attianus may have been no more than fanciful. To remove him from the powerful post of command of the praetorians, Hadrian adlected him into the senate with consular rank, but Attianus never held a consulate, nor was he ever governor of a province, as far as we can tell.

15.2 *Nepotem*  See 4.2

15.2 *Septicium Clarum*  See 9.5

15.3 *Eudaemonem*  Perhaps Valerius Eudaemon, who had a long life marked by vicissitudes. An *eques* of Egyptian origin, he served Hadrian as *procurator ad dioecesin Alexandriae*, as procurator of both the Greek and Latin libraries, and as procurator of numerous provinces: Lycia, Pamphylia, Galatia, Paphlagonia, Pisidia, Pontus, Asia, and Syria. In addition, before his service in Asia, he was *procurator hereditatum*. We do not know what caused the break with the emperor, in consequence of which Eudaemon was reduced to poverty, and, we may assume, disgrace. But he survived, and held high office once again under Antoninus. His fall from favor probably, therefore, came late in Hadrian's reign. See Pflaum (1) #110.

15.4 *Polyaenum*  Neither this emended name nor the MS reading Polenus produces any person known to history. Perhaps the corruption conceals the name of Ti. Iulius Aquila Polemaeanus, *cos. suff.* 110, who was responsible for the completion and dedication of the splendid library begun by his father, Ti. Iulius Celsus Polemaeanus (*cos. suff.* 92), in Ephesus. If this is indeed the person meant in the text, he lived at least to the beginning of Hadrian's reign; the reason for his suicide is unknown.

15.4 *Marcellum*   Probably L. Neratius Marcellus, *cos. suff.* in 95 and *cos. II ord.* in 129, very late in life. He was legate of Britain in 103; the length of his tenure is unknown. While he was governor, Pliny requested a military tribunate for Suetonius from him, but when it was granted Suetonius did not take it up and it was transferred to someone else. Later in the reign of Trajan, Neratius served as *curator aquarum urbis*, an important post which had been earlier held by the eminent Frontinus. He must have been on good terms with Hadrian to have been granted a second consulship, although he held no official posts under him as far as we know. It therefore seems surprising that he was driven to suicide. One might conjecture that he chose to end his life because of disease, and the author has failed to distinguish voluntary and enforced death.

If the above identification is correct, he is the brother of L. Neratius Priscus (see 4.8).

An alternate candidate is C. Quinctius Certus Poblicius (or Publicius) Marcellus. He was suffect consul in 120, became an augur, was legate of Germania superior during the decade of the 120s, and was legate of Syria for an extended period. His tenure is confirmed in 130/1, although he may have taken up his position in an earlier year, and he continued to serve until 134/5, although, for a brief period during that span, he was relieved by another; the reason for this unusual arrangement is unknown, unless it was to give Marcellus a more direct appointment against the Jews. For his success against them, he was honored with the *ornamenta triumphalia*.

He outlived the emperor (*AE* 1934, 231).

15.5 *Heliodorum*   C. Avidius Heliodorus was an Epicurean philosopher. Born in Syria, he served Hadrian as *ab epistulis Graecis*, was prefect of Egypt at the beginning of 138 (thus at the very end of Hadrian's reign), and is further known as the father of Avidius Cassius, who rose in revolt against Marcus in 175 and lost his life in the attempt. In 16.10, it is stated that Hadrian held Heliodorus *in summa familiaritate*, here that he attacked him *famosissimis litteris*. Some, as Pflaum, deny the possibility of both passages referring to the same man; others, as Bowersock, see no difficulty whatever: "A philosopher-rhetor should evoke no surprise." Dio LXIX 3.5 tells us of an occasion when Dionysius of Miletus, himself an eminent sophist, chid Heliodorus, "Caesar can give you money and honor, but he cannot make you an orator."

If all these references concern one man, and I think they
do, then the occasion which brought forth Hadrian's attack had
no lasting consequence on Heliodorus' career. See Pflaum (1)
#106; Bowersock (1) 50-1.

15.6 *Titianum* The biography of Antoninus reports (7.3):
*publicatio bonorum rarior quam umquam fuit, ita ut unus tantum
proscriberetur affectatae tyrannidis reus, hoc est Atilius
Titianus, senatu puniente, a quo conscios requiri vetuit, filio
eius ad omnia semper adiuto.* This is so similar to the present
passage that it appears to be a doublet. Or are we dealing with
two distinct but similar events in the life of one man, or perhaps with a father and son? The full name is T. Atilius Rufus
Titianus; he was *consul ordinarius* in 127. Clearly he had
Hadrian's favor up to that point; was the indicated grasp at
power late in the reign, when the emperor was beginning to think
of a successor? If the same man is the subject of both passages,
he was convicted and exiled under Hadrian, recalled by Antoninus,
and then once again proscribed. That does not mean he was put
to death.

15.7 *Umidium Quadratum* Cos. suff. in 118, with Hadrian as colleague, this man was the scion of an important family. He may
have been proconsul of Africa in 133/4. His son married Annia
Cornificia Faustina, Marcus' sister. Hadrian's enmity may have
arisen from Quadratus' consequent involvement in the intrigues
of succession. It is certain, however, that he did not lose his
life in consequence. For this remarkably long-surviving family,
which endured from the principate of Tiberius to the late third
century, see Syme (10); the present Quadratus is discussed 84-98.

15.7 *Catilium Severum* See 5.10

15.7 *Turbonem* See 4.2. To the details of his career sketched
there may be added the statement that we do not know when he
died. It does not appear that he was put to death by Hadrian,
nor do we know whether the implied disfavor led to his ultimate
removal from high office.

15.8 *Servianum* Servianus has already been mentioned twice in
the *vita*, in a substantive way: his enmity to Hadrian in the
latter's youth is detailed in 2.6 and the emperor's respect for
him, as well as his attainment of a third consulate, in 8.11.
(His presence as one of the consuls cited in 3.8 is an error;

*quod vide*.)   His enforced death is mentioned three additional times:   23.2, 23.8, and 25.8.

We know nothing of his career before his first consulate in 90; he was then about 43 years old. His name at that point was Ser. Iulius Servianus. He was legate of Germania superior in 97/98, moved to Pannonia in 98, where he stayed until the end of 100, served with Trajan in the first Dacian war in 101-102, and became *consul II ordinarius* in 102. His name at this point is L. Iulius Ursus Servianus, which suggests adoption at some time before this year by L. Iulius Ursus, who was consul for the third time in 100. Servianus will undoubtedly have received enormous political advantage from this relationship. No further military commands or provincial posts are known; finally, in the fulness of years, aged about 87, he receives a third consulate, only the second man so honored during the principate of his brother-in-law. It is hard, therefore, to credit the report of Hadrian's enmity toward him, at this late time, on the grounds that he was an *affectator imperii* (23.8), unless thereby is meant maneuvering on behalf of his grandson, Pedanius Fuscus (see 23.3). Dio LXIX 17.3 reports that Hadrian had considered him worthy of rule (*capax imperii*): "for instance, Hadrian had once at a banquet told his friends to name him ten men who were competent to be sole ruler, and then, after a moment's pause, had added: 'Nine only I want to know; for one I have already-- Servianus.'" But an alternative reading for Hadrian's name is that of Trajan, and that perhaps makes more sense. Trajan and Servianus were not very far apart in age, while Servianus was almost thirty years older than Hadrian. In addition, Hadrian may have nourished continuing resentment against the older man for the slights and difficulties the latter had put in his path in his own early career (2.6), unless they are mere scandal.

15.9  *libertos et milites*   No names are known, if indeed this statement is true.

15.10  *promtissimus et peritissimus*   See 3.11, 14.9, 25.9

15.10-11  *risit, contempsit, obtrivit, certavit*   See 16.8

15.12  *Favorinus*   An eminent philosopher and sophist. Born in Arles, as an hermaphrodite, he became, by choice, one of the great figures of the Greek renaissance of the second century. He enjoyed Hadrian's favor, but nonetheless had his disagreements with the emperor, on matters of the intellect, as here, as well

as on more substantive matters. In a trial in which he claimed
immunity from a public duty, he gave in after learning that
Hadrian was opposed to his claim. Hadrian promoted his enemy to
damage his status (Dio LXIX 3.4) and may have sent him into
exile on an island, perhaps Chios. His work *De exilio* probably
refers to this. But he survived well into the reign of Antoninus.

Philostratus *VS* I 8 (489), the chief source for Favorinus'
life, reports: "Though he quarreled with the Emperor Hadrian, he
suffered no ill consequences. Hence he used to say in the ambiguous style of an oracle, that there were in the story of his life
these three paradoxes: Though he was a Gaul he led the life of
a Hellene; a eunuch, he had been tried for adultery; he had
quarreled with an Emperor and was still alive." See 16.10

16.1 *libros vitae suae*  See 1.1. P. Aelius Phlegon was a learned
man, whose origin was Tralles. Extensive fragments of his own
historical work survive (*FGrH* II 257).

16.2 *catacannas*  The word itself is insecure in the manuscripts;
it may refer to abundance and luxuriance or to a kind of medley,
satirical or ironical in tone. The obscurity may have been due
to Hadrian himself, rather than his model, although Antimachus
was not noted for his clarity. His life spanned the last half
of the fifth century into the beginning of the fourth; a scholar
as much as a poet, his style, as far as can be judged, was prolix
and tedious. He wrote long works, of epic character. Hadrian's
choice of him as an antecedent is perhaps more surprising than
his favorites in Latin literature (see 16.6), for he was never
a major figure.

Marcus uses the word in a letter to Fronto (*ad M. Caes.*
II 11; Haines I 140-1), referring to a tree with many branches.

16.3 *Floro*  Three Floruses are known, an historian, a rhetorician, and a poet. Modern scholarship tends to combine the three
into one, by name P. Annius Florus or L. Annaeus Florus. Among
his works are a condensation of Roman history based upon Livy
and a verse epic celebrating Trajan's Dacian triumph. The gentile
name Annaeus suggests possible relation with the family of Seneca
and hence Spanish origin; that he spent much of his adult life
in Tarraco is known. He clearly was on friendly and intimate
terms with Hadrian, else the flippant tone of these verses and
the emperor's reply would hardly have been possible. See Schanz-
Hosius 67-73.

The MSS furnish only three verses for Florus, four for Hadrian. This seems unlikely, for each of Florus' verses is exactly matched by one of Hadrian's; there must have been a third line beginning *latitare*. One suggestion has been to insert *latitare per Achivos*.

This would give a proper noun in each of the last three lines, which Hadrian then capped with a common noun of humorous and insulting import in each instance. Such regularity need not be demanded; *Britannos* and *Scythicas* imply the furthest reaches of the empire and its frontiers, regions marked by weather anything but Mediterranean. *Achivos* does not fit this pattern; it refers to a land and people whom the emperor highly esteemed, warm and cultured. Perhaps something like *latitare per paludes*.

16.5 *genus vetustum dicendi* Hadrian's taste clearly ran to the archaic, as exemplified by the three pairs of authors immediately presented, representing respectively oratory, epic, and history. Cato, Ennius, and Coelius Antipater all flourished in the second century B.C. No mention of Tacitus, whom Hadrian must surely have known, and who had surpassed Sallust. To prefer Coelius "is enough to condemn him." (Syme [6] 249.)

16.5 *controversias* Rhetorical training in the first century A.D. focused upon two types of discourse, *suasoriae* and *controversiae*. Both tended to treat fantastic themes and difficult points of law, the former being monologues, the latter debates. The Elder Seneca is our best source for these exercises; for criticism of this form of education, see Tac. *Dial*. 31-32. See Kennedy 314-22.

16.6 *Homero ac Platone* Homer found no favor with Hadrian, but was supplanted by the epic writer Antimachus of Colophon, praised by Alexandrian grammarians but long since forgotten. Many knew not even his name when Hadrian championed him (Dio LXIX 4.6). About Plato there is no particular statement; clearly he too was supplanted by a lesser figure in esteem. This was the age of the Greek revival, known as the Second Sophistic; the emperor, dubbed the *Graeculus*, was its active and spiritual head. See T. B. Jones and Bowersock (1).

16.7 *mathesin* The source of this notice is clearly Marius Maximus, who is cited in a parallel context in the life of Aelius (3.9): *fuisse enim Hadrianum peritum matheseos Marius Maximus usque adeo demonstrat, ut eum dicat cuncta de se scisse, sic ut omnium dierum usque ad horam mortis futuros actus ante perscripserit.* Astrology was very popular in the early empire, with Tiberius the best known practitioner (Tac. *Ann.* VI 20.2-21). Gellius XIV 1 reports a long discourse by Favorinus (see 15.12) against the Chaldaeans and the whole idea of prophesy. *Astrologi* are included among the *doctores* with whom Hadrian associated (16.10-11). See 2.4. For discussion of the entire subject, see Cramer.

16.8 *reprehendendis* See 15.10-11

16.8 *grammaticis, rhetoribus* Both the *grammaticus* and the *rhetor* dealt with "higher education." The former was concerned with language and literature, and took the exposition of both prose and poetry for his province, but particularly the latter. The rhetorician taught the art of oratory, and thus basically limited himself to prose, except for the poetry which could give oratory a special sheen, as Tacitus records in *Dial.* 20.5-6, speaking of *poeticus cultus* and *poeticus decor*. The two classes of scholar were parallel in prestige; both were included in the honorific grouping of *professores*.

16.8 *quaestionibus* See 20.2

16.10 *Epictetum* The eminent Stoic philosopher. Born a slave in Phrygia, he studied with Musonius Rufus, was subsequently freed, and, under Domitian, left Rome because of the decree of the senate expelling philosophers from Rome and Italy. He moved to Nicopolis in Epirus and lived and taught there for the remainder of his life. An intimate friend of Hadrian, as indicated here, he was also on close terms with Antoninus and Marcus. He may have survived into the latter's principate.

His pupil Arrian collected his discourses and published them; four books have survived. His influence on Marcus was significant. See 20.2

16.10 *Heliodorum* See 15.5

16.10 *Favorino* See 15.12

16.11 *doctores* Victor 14.2-3 relates: *caerimonias leges gymnasia doctoresque curare occepit, adeo quidem, ut etiam ludum ingenuarum artium, quod Athenaeum vocant, constitueret.*

Vespasian had established the first state-supported chairs of Latin and Greek rhetoric, with Quintilian the first appointee

to the former. The emperor could impose his choice not only upon
these positions but any other that might concern him, and we can
be sure that Hadrian kept close watch on the teaching posts in
the major cities of the empire. Many of these learned sophists
were well known to him, often acting as ambassadors for their
native cities, and his unfavorable response to their efforts or
personal dislike could lead to their dismissal.

17.1 *capitalem* = *inimicissimum*

17.3 *saturnalicia et sigillaricia* The former were presents
given during the festival of the *Saturnalia*, which ran for about
a week from December 17. It was a period of great joy and
license for slaves, marked by an exchange of gifts, *saturnalicia*,
among which were small statuettes, *sigillaricia*. The range of
gifts given at this time was impressive; there are literary references to clay figures, marble figures, Corinthian bronzes,
statues of silver or gold, pictures, other works of art, clothes,
and carpets.

17.3 *inopinantibus* See 15.1

17.4 *obsonatorum fraudes* In polite company, all guests were
served the same food and wine. Mean hosts varied the quality of
the meal depending upon the rank of the guest, so that poor
clients, when invited, gazed upon the best of food and drink but
were themselves served inferior stuff. This was a practice
against which Juvenal railed (*Sat.* V), and Pliny the Younger
similarly took offense at it (*Ep.* II 6.3): *eadem omnibus pono:
ad cenam enim, non ad notam invito cunctisque rebus exaequo, quos
mensa et toro aequavi.* Hadrian evidently could not trust members
of his own household staff to furnish all guests the same food.

17.4 *simmatibus* i.e. *sigmatibus* The triclinium contained room
for three couches, upon each of which three persons could recline.
When a dinner gathering was larger than nine, the normal thing
was to use two or more adjacent triclinia, but occasionally any
number of couches could be placed in a large room in the pattern
of the Greek lunate sigma, in a horseshoe arrangement.

17.5 *muneribus* The first part of the chapter, through 17.9,
describes Hadrian's private behavior, as an emperor who displayed
the varied aspects of *civilitas* (see 20.1). The *munera* mentioned
here, therefore, are not to be confused with those which played
a part in diplomacy (17.10-12). The former were regal in scale

Commentary 109

and scope, and are to be linked with the *saturnalicia et sigillaricia* mentioned earlier. This sentence would be more meaningful if it followed the former more closely, without a break dealing with a diverse subject.

17.5 *lavit* Bathing in public was not a practice followed by his predecessors, save for one exception, Titus (Suet. *Tit.* 8.2): *ne quid popularitatis praetermitteret, nonnumquam in thermis suis admissa plebe lavit.* This was part of Hadrian's feeling that, as an individual, he was no better than his fellow man; for other examples of such behavior, see 9.7-8 and 20.1.

17.6 *veteranum notum* See 10.8, 20.10

17.8 *plebis iactantissimus amator* The words suggest that Hadrian cultivated the favor of the common people in ways that were perhaps not suitable to an emperor. This might be because his relations with the senate were damaged early in his reign by the affair of the four consulars (see 7.1-2). The adjective also tends to be pejorative. But that need not be; E. Birley (3) 89 notes: "under *amare* Lessing's Lexicon registers frequent cases in which that verb indicates the feelings of people for their rulers." The words might therefore be rendered, "he was very proud of being beloved by the common people."

17.8 *peregrinationis ita cupidus* For his travels, more extensive than those of any of his predecessors, which kept him away from Italy for more than half his reign and took him to almost every province of the empire, see 13.5 and App. IV. See also Dio LXIX 9, and note Fronto's comment: *Eius itinerum monumenta videas per plurimas Asiae atque Europae urbes sita* (*Principia Historiae* 10, Haines II 206).

17.8 *addiscere* Not only get to know first hand, but later to reproduce, in part, at his villa at Tibur (see 26.5).

17.9 *caput* See 23.1. Dio LXIX 9.4 reports that "He covered his head neither in hot weather nor in cold, but alike amid German snows and under scorching Egyptian suns he went about with his head bare."

17.10 *regibus multis* This and the following section paint a basically uncomplimentary picture of Hadrian's foreign policy, with peace and security won not by force of arms or prestige, but by gifts and favors. Dacia, of course, was not given up (see

5.3), and there were wars and campaigns, but in the east diplomacy carried the day. Cf. 21.10-13. See Stroheker 246.

*Epit.* 14.10 speaks similarly: *A regibus multis pace occultius muneribus impetrata, iactabat palam plus se otio adeptum quam armis ceteros.*

17.10 *nonnullis* Pharasmanes is the only such person mentioned (13.9, 17.12).

17.11 *Hiberorum* Their king was Pharasmanes; see 13.9.

17.11 *quinquagenariam cohortem* If correct, the reading means a unit of fifty men, which corresponds to no regular unit in the Roman army. But if the numerical adjective is read as *quingenariam*, then there is reference to a regular infantry unit of five hundred men, a quingenary cohort.

17.12 *Farasmane* See 13.9

17.12 *munia* This word is perhaps corrupted from *munera*, as in 17.11, and means the same thing as *dona*. Excision or emendation seems necessary, unless we assume an attempt at emphasis by use of two synonyms; in that case, we should expect a connective.

17.12 *in harenam* The criminals were condemned to fight as gladiators.

18.1 *iudicaret* The administration of justice was one of the main features of Hadrian's principate, marked by his close relationship with eminent jurists. He "was the first emperor to defend the weak against the strong, the poor against the rich, the 'humiliores' against the 'honestiores,' the 'tenuiores' against the 'potentiores.'" (Pringsheim 143) To discuss particular measures within a larger context is beyond the scope of the present commentary. A full survey of his reforms, rescripts, and responses is found in Hänel 85-101; they are presented chronologically, where a date can be determined, and, of course, many of the items are taken from this *Vita*. For a discussion, see Pringsheim. See 8.1 and 8.9

18.1 *in consilio habuit* An emperor's *consilium* was made up, above all, of men whom he trusted, once the initial attempt at a "cabinet," instituted by Augustus, had fallen by the wayside. Holders of specific offices and others chosen by lot from the senate served for six months and assisted the emperor in the

establishment of policy and the preparation of legislation.  But
after Augustus, the emperor's *consilium* was a private amenity.
Indeed, the term *consilium principis* is not found in antiquity.
Yet the need for advice on every emperor's part was beyond cavil,
and the most obvious candidates to aid him were his friends.  But
surely here one should assume that *amici aut comites* and *iuris
consulti* were not mutually exclusive classes; Hadrian preferred
men of legal background who were his friends.  Nor should one
assume that he allowed the senate to pass upon those whom he
wished to consult.  That would give the senate a kind of veto
which it did not possess.  See, in general, Crook (1) 56-65 and
Hammond (3) 370-82.

18.1 *Iuventium Celsum*  He is the only one of the trio here mentioned who reached the distinction of a second consulate.  The
son of a P. Iuventius Celsus, himself a jurist, he was evidently
adopted into the family of T. Aufidius Hoenius Severus, so that
his own name becomes P. Iuventius Celsus T. Aufidius Hoenius
Severianus.  He was *legatus Augusti pro praetore* of Thrace in
114, *cos. suff.* probably in 115, *cos. II ord.* in 129, and proconsul of Asia in 129/30.  His colleague in 129 was Neratius
Marcellus, similarly celebrating a second consulship, the
brother of the jurist mentioned in this same line.

18.1 *Salvium Iulianum*  A prodigy in the field of Roman law.  Born
about 100, he was honored by Hadrian with double salary, when
the emperor's quaestor, *propter insignem doctrinam* (Smallwood
236, for the fullest indication of his career), and, when still
younger than thirty, was charged by Hadrian with the enormously
complex task of culling all past praetorian edicts and producing
an *edictum perpetuum*.  He wrote much else, with ninety books of
*Digesta* his most important work.  He was consul in 148, and lived
to about 170.  His full name is L. Octavius Cornelius P. Salvius
Julianus Aemilianus.

"Julian is perhaps the most remarkable representative of
Roman jurisprudence.  It may justifiably be claimed that Roman
legal science reached in him the height of its development.  The
Severan jurists, Ulpianus, Papinianus, and Paulus, surpassed him
in the volume and encyclopedic character of their writings, but
he had the greater originality and creative power, and exercised
a more formative influence on the law." (*OCD*$^2$ 568)

18.1 *Neratium Priscum*  See 4.8

18.2 *domus aliqua . . . dirueretur* That a building be routinely destroyed was an act that Roman law frowned upon. Three municipal charters, of the first centuries B.C. and A.D., which undoubtedly reflect the custom and law of Rome, prohibit the destruction of buildings. These are the charters of Tarentum (Riccobono *FIRA* I 18), Urso (*FIRA* I 21), and Malaga (*FIRA* I 24). In addition, there have survived two *senatusconsulta de aedificiis diruendis* (*FIRA* I 45), as well as a letter of Hadrian to the citizens of Stratonicaea, recently renamed Hadrianopolis (see 20.4), of the year 127, in which he orders that the owner of a dilapidated house either repair it or sell it to a fellow citizen who will (Smallwood 453). But nowhere else do we find mention of demolition of a building in order to carry the material off to another city. It would seem that the costs of transport would render such a practice uneconomical; nonetheless, if it did exist, Hadrian expanded the law against destruction of buildings by prohibiting their being cannibalized for their fabric.

18.3 *liberis proscriptorum* In Roman law, conviction on a capital charge entailed loss of property, as well as the major penalty of death or exile. But this, of course, left the family destitute, and did particular disservice to the sons, who would have no hope of a political career without the appropriate census. Tacitus twice records (*Ann.* III 17.4, XIII 43.5) that the children of those condemned received half the property. Thus, when our author speaks of Hadrian granting twelfth shares, this can hardly be the norm; it must be considered a minimum, with half remaining the usual portion. A rescript of Marcus and Verus is reported (*Dig.* XLVIII 20.1) on this subject: *Damnatione bona publicantur, cum aut vita adimitur aut civitas, aut servilis condicio irrogatur. Etiam si qui ante concepti et post damnationem nati sunt, portiones ex bonis patrum damnatorum accipiunt. Liberis autem ita demum portio tribuitur, si iustis nuptiis nati sint. Liberis eius, cui pars dimidia dumtaxat bonorum ablata est, partes non dantur.*

Dio LXIX 23.3 relates that "If it was absolutely necessary to punish any man who had children, yet in proportion to the number of his children he would lighten the penalty imposed."

18.4 *maiestatis crimina* The story of the "treason" laws produces one of the less happy pages of Rome's imperial history. Tac. *Ann.* I 72.2 pinpoints Tiberius' action in "bringing back" the law of treason as the beginning of an unmitigated evil. During the republic, although the Lex Cornelia of Sulla had included libel in the definition of *maiestas, ne in quemvis impune declamari liceret* (Cic. *Fam.* III 11.2), freedom of speech was hardly impaired. But, as Tacitus said, other actions were the concern of the treason laws: *si quis proditione exercitum aut plebem seditionibus, denique male gesta re publica maiestatem populi Romani minuisset: facta arguebantur, dicta impune erant. primus Augustus cognitionem de famosis libellis specie legis eius tractavit.*

Much turmoil ensued through the remainder of the first century A.D. in consequence, although not with consistency from reign to reign. The emperors from Nerva to Marcus were exemplary in their response to *maiestas* cases; basically, they did not receive them at all, as is stated here of Hadrian. For a full study, see Bauman.

18.5 *hereditates* From Augustus onward, the emperors received enormous amounts of money and property from the wills of friends and subjects (in this sense, the two are not meant to be identical). In twenty years, prior to the writing of his own will in 13 A.D., Augustus received 1,400,000,000 sesterces from the wills of friends, and was pleased by their remembrance. But, under worse emperors, such as Nero and Domitian, it was considered foresight to declare the emperor joint heir with one's own relations, hoping thereby to secure confirmation of the will and the retention of at least part of the property within the family. Domitian rejoiced in having been named joint heir by Agricola, not realizing how that action marked him (Tac. *Agr.*43.4): *satis constabat lecto testamento Agricolae, quo coheredem optimae uxori et piissimae filiae Domitianum scripsit, laetatum eum velut honore iudicioque. tam caeca et corrupta mens adsiduis adulationibus erat, ut nesciret a bono patre non scribi heredem nisi malum principem.*

Trajan's practice was in marked contrast, according to Pliny *Pan.* 43.2: *scriberis ab amicis, ab ignotis praeteriris, nihilque inter privatum et principem interest, nisi quod nunc a pluribus amaris; nam et plures amas.*

Hadrian chose to follow Trajan and the other "good" emperors in considering that being named as an heir in a will should be a mark of friendship and respect from one who was at least an acquaintance and that blood heirs should not have their property diminished by the addition of others.

18.6 *de thesauris* This is an accurate statement (*Inst.* II 1.39): *Thesauros, quos quis in suo loco invenerit, divus*

*Hadrianus naturalem aequitatem secutus ei concessit qui invenerit, idemque statuit, si quis in sacro aut in religioso loco fortuito casu invenerit. at si quis in alieno loco non data ad hoc opera, sed fortuitu invenerit, dimidium domino soli concessit. et convenienter, si quis in Caesaris loco invenerit, dimidium inventoris, dimidium Caesaris esse statuit.*

Roman law considered not only money but also jewels and bullion and anything hidden in the ground as treasure. Note that the imperial decisions concern accidental finds; intended discoveries went to the owner of the land.

18.7 *servos* The lot of slaves had become increasingly milder during the empire, with much impetus from Stoic philosophy, which supported the essential sameness of all men. Claudius had been responsible for legislation which freed slaves who had been exposed to die because of ill health and then recovered. A rescript of Hadrian to Sennius Sabinus is quoted by Ulpian (*Dig.* XLVIII 18.1.1): *Ad tormenta servorum ita demum veniri oportet, cum suspectus est reus et aliis argumentis ita probationi admovetur, ut sola confessio servorum deesse videatur.* Similarly, in a rescript to Claudius Quartinus, he ordered: *a suspectissimo incipiendum et a quo facillime posse verum scire iudex crediderit.*

18.9 *decoctores* Surprisingly, the narrative concerned with slaves is broken by the insertion of two items which are unrelated: the punishment of those who wasted their property and the separation of the sexes in public bathing. The passage has been inelegantly constructed.

Hadrian's punishment of prodigals was novel and severe. Earlier, such a man suffered no penalty from the state, other than being assigned to a particular seating area in the theater, which would shame him. Now prodigality became a state offense.

18.10 *ergastula* The *ergastulum* was a feature of slave labor, a kind of dungeon, usually semi-subterranean, used either as a place of punishment or where certain kinds of slaves were regularly confined. These last were normally those with sufficient strength to cause difficulty. Since slaves were such an important part of the functioning of Roman society, free men were often kidnapped and sold into slavery. Both Augustus and Tiberius undertook to prevent the detention of free men in *ergastula*, but Hadrian here is credited with elimination of the place and the practice. See Fitzgibbon.

18.11 *lavacra* Mixed bathing was never anything but exceptional at Rome and in the empire. The public bathing establishments normally had two sets of identical rooms, commonly sharing the furnace area, for the two sexes. The men's quarters were usually larger and frequently included a palaestra, which the women did not always enjoy. If the baths did not provide separate quarters, there were separate times of use, with the women customarily having several mornings each week. Yet there is evidence that mixed bathing did occur, particularly under the more licentious emperors, and hence such imperial measures as Hadrian's were periodically necessary. See 22.7

18.11 *si dominus in domo interemptus esset* This sentence records a significant relaxation of long-standing practice. An Augustan *senatus consultum* had required that, if a master were murdered, his entire household was to be put to death; another of Neronian date included freedmen among those punishable. The murder of the city prefect Pedanius Secundus in 61 led to a violent debate in the senate and reaffirmation of the inclusive death penalty for all slaves. A riot on the part of the people required Nero to post troops so that the death sentence could be inflicted. See Tac. *Ann.* XIV 42-45.

19.1 *praeturam* All the offices mentioned in this paragraph are the chief magistracies in various municipalities, colonies, and cities throughout the empire, not that all possibilities are here enumerated. Normally, all the offices other than that of *dictator* were collegial, but when the emperor held the office he had no colleague, and actually carried out the duties of office through a *praefectus*. Naples retained its Greek character right through the empire; we have the testimony of both Strabo (V 4.7) and Tacitus (*Ann.* XV 33.2), who tells of Nero's choice of the Campanian city for his first public appearance as an artist: *non tamen Romae incipere ausus Neapolim quasi Graecam urbem delegit.*

The census had to be taken every fifth year; the local chief magistracy was thus more significant than usual during that year, and the official was styled *quinquennalis*. It would appear that Hadrian felt a measure of local pride in being *quinquennalis* in both Italica and Hadria. The archonship at Athens must have ranked with his initiation into the Eleusinian mysteries in giving him pleasure (see 13.1). He is the only known private Roman citizen to have been archon; the date was 112 (See App. II).

Since he never visited Italica after becoming emperor (see 12.4), he must have held his office there *in absentia*.

**19.2** *aliquid aedificavit* *Epit.* 14.4-5 speaks of his extraordinary building activity in the provinces, *cum oppida universa restitueret . . . Namque ad specimen legionum militarium fabros perpendiculatores architectos genusque cunctum exstruendorum moenium seu decorandorum in cohortes centuriaverat*. These men were part of his retinue, and he furnished their expert services to the various communities that required them, as well as undertaking many buildings *de novo*.

**19.4** *avocavit* The verb indicates that he made use of local talent when he put on hunts and plays elsewhere than at Rome.

**19.5** *socrus suae* See 9.9

**19.6** *fabulas omnis generis* The use of the words *more antiquo* recalls Hadrian's archaic preferences (see 16.6). The dramas undoubtedly include comedies and tragedies, both on Greek and Roman subjects, as well as the artistic form most popular in the age, pantomime. This was the emperor's public taste; in private it was the same, and is spelled out more explicitly in 26.4.

**19.6** *publicavit* He permitted the actors belonging to the imperial household to perform for the general public.

**19.8** *militares pyrrichas* Dances performed in armor, normally by young men.

**19.9** *numquam ipse nisi in Traiani patris templo nomen suum scripsit* Trajan's Forum, the last and largest of the five imperial fora, was the only one of which the original plan omitted a temple. Caesar had built a temple to Venus Genetrix, Augustus one to Mars Ultor, Vespasian one to Pax, Domitian one to Minerva, but the dominating building of Trajan's complex was the Basilica Ulpia, behind which stood the famous column and the two flanking libraries. After the deaths first of Trajan and then Plotina, Hadrian rectified the omission, constructing a temple to the two *divi* beyond the column; what was inscribed on the architrave is unknown, but another inscription has survived (Smallwood 141): *[E]x s.c. divi[s Tr]aiano Parthico et [Plotinae im]p. Caes[ar di]vi Traiani Parthici [f.] divi*

N[ervae nepos Traia]nus Hadrianus Aug. pont· m[ax. trib. pot.--]
cos. III parentibus sui[s].

19.10 *Pantheum* The building existing today is totally
Hadrianic; throughout its fabric are bricks with stamps from
his reign. The original building of Agrippa, whose inscription
of the year 27 B.C. survives on the architrave, was probably a
regular rectangular temple. Hadrian began *de novo*, with a design
that was very likely his own. He wished to house all the
official divinities of the empire in this one temple, dedicated
to all. See MacDonald.

19.10 *saepta* This was an enormous building in the Campus
Martius for the holding of elections, begun by Julius Caesar,
continued by the triumvir Lepidus, and completed by Agrippa.
It was more than 300 meters long, about 95 meters wide, and
flanked on its two long sides by porticoes. It was put to a
variety of uses under the empire when the people no longer participated in elections. The great fire of 80 damaged it, but
it was soon restored; what misfortune caused Hadrian's restoration, we do not know.

19.10 *basilicam Neptuni* Built by Agrippa in 25 B.C., as a
memorial of his naval victories over Sextus Pompeius at Mylae in
36 and over Marcus Antonius and Cleopatra at Actium in 31, it
was located directly south of the Pantheon and west of the
Saepta. Its restoration perhaps came about as part of Hadrian's
major undertaking in this part of the Campus Martius.

19.10 *sacras aedes plurimas* This statement seems excessive.
In addition to the temple of the Bona Dea mentioned in the next
section, there is record of only four religious structures
which Hadrian repaired or reconstructed: the *aedicula Vestae*,
the *templum Divi Iulii*, the *templum Divi Augusti*, and the
*auguratorium*.

19.10 *forum Augusti* The second of the imperial fora, this
great complex was dedicated in 2 B.C. It was dominated by the
temple of Mars Ultor, and contained in its flanking porticoes
and exedrae statues of the great figures of Rome's past, thus
constituting a Hall of Fame. We do not know what Hadrian did to
the forum; he may have wished to link himself with the founder
of the empire in this way, as in so many others (see 22.10).

19.10 *lavacrum Agrippae*  If the name is correct, this is the only extant reference to these baths, and it has consequently been proposed to alter the name to *Agrippinae*; this monument is independently known. But it seems much easier and more sensible to assume that *lavacrum* is used in place of *thermae*; if so, this refers to the first great public baths in Rome, built in 25 B.C., and located just to the west of the Pantheon. Hadrian's labors here will then be linked with the general restoration of the area based upon the reconstruction of the Pantheon.

19.11 *pontem et sepulchrum*  These are the *pons Aelius* and the *mausoleum Hadriani*; the latter was built on the other side of the Tiber, opposite the Campus Martius. The bridge was completed in 134, the mausoleum not until 139. The latter is better known today as the Castel San Angelo, and its present appearance displays its later history as both fortress and palace.

19.11 *aedem Bonae Deae*  This was located on the Aventine. It is curious that this little known and relatively unimportant temple merits specific mention from the author, rather than being subsumed in the general notice of the preceding section. We know of no special relationship that Hadrian had with this divinity.

19.12-13 *colossum*  This statue of Nero, estimated to have been some 35 meters high, was a dominant feature of his enormous residential complex known as the *domus aurea*, which stretched from the southern limit of the Palatine to the heights of the Esquiline. After Nero's death, much of it was destroyed or put to other use: Vespasian built the great amphitheatre known as the Colosseum on the site of a lake, Titus built public baths higher up the hill. Hadrian chose the heights of the Velia, adjacent to the arch of Titus and across a valley from the amphitheatre, for the largest temple ever built in Rome, the Temple of Venus and Rome. It required removal of the colossus to the valley, an enormous task of engineering, entrusted to Decrianus, of whom nothing else is known.

Apollodorus of Damascus was Trajan's great military and civic architect and engineer. He built the bridge over the Danube and was responsible for the forum of Trajan and the column in Rome, along with other major projects. Whether he undertook the statue in honor of the moon, or only suggested it, is unclear from the Latin. Dio LXIX 4 tells that Hadrian

developed a dislike for him and ultimately had him put to
death. The antipathy between the two may have stemmed from
differing outlooks between the professional architect and the
gifted amateur. Hadrian was responsible for the design of his
own buildings.

The *templum Urbis* mentioned here is an alternate name for
the *templum Veneris et Romae*. The text appears defective after
*vultum*; a participle seems necessary.

20.1 *civilissimus* The words *civilis*, *civiliter*, and *civilitas*
were much favored by Tacitus and Suetonius, particularly with
political connotations. In the principate, the words refer to
relations of the emperors with other members of the state
according to the model of the citizens of the republic. For
Tacitus, at first, when an emperor was *civilis*, it meant that he
refused excessive honors, respected wills, did not transgress
the prerogatives of magistrates and the senate, retained republican practices with regard to the people, and did not claim
privileges for himself or for others of the court. The word
meant much more than affable behavior, for which he used
*comis/comiter*. But in the second half of the *Annals*, *civilis*
loses its political connotation, and becomes parallel to *comis*.

This is the meaning which our author intends here. Hadrian
enjoyed mixing with the people (see 9.7-8 and 17.5), and resented
the animadversions of those who thought that his affability
demeaned the prestige and power of the princeps. "Never reluc-
tant to encounter his inferiors, Hadrian comported himself with
ease as any man's equal. . . . Both his words and his behaviour
let it be known that he did not set a high value on class and
rank." (Syme [2] 249, 487)

20.2 *quaestiones* There survives a set of twenty questions
which Hadrian put to Secundus of Athens, who was known as "The
Silent Philosopher" because he had taken an oath not to speak.
Whether historical or not, they appear to typify the kind of
intellectual discourse which delighted the emperor and frequently
led to the embarrassment of the professional scholar (see 16.8).
The first question was     τί ἐστι κόσμος;      The twenty
subjects were the world, ocean, god, day, sun, moon, man,
woman, wealth, poverty, friend, old age, sleep, beauty, earth,
farmer, gladiator, ship, sailor, and death.

Similar is the *Altercatio Hadriani Augusti et Epicteti
Philosophi*, which is a series of seventy-three questions and

answers. For text and discussion, see Daly and Suchier; for
Secundus, see Perry. For Epictetus, see 16.10.

20.3 *Marius Maximus*   See 2.10

20.3 *quod Domitiano accidit*   Domitian, of course, was assassi-
nated, in spite of his fears and elaborate precautions. Suet.
*Dom.* 21.1 reports his apropos statement: *condicionem principum
miserrimam aiebat, quibus de coniuratione comperta non
crederetur nisi occisis.* Our author recalls this in a letter
of Marcus to Verus about the aspirations of Avidius Cassius
(*AC* 2.5-6): *scis enim ipse, quid avus tuus Hadrianus dixerit:
"misera conditio imperatorum, quibus de affectata tyrannide nisi
occisis non potest credi." eius autem exemplum ponere malui
quam Domitiani, qui hoc primus dixisse fertur; tyrannorum enim
etiam bona dicta non habent tantum auctoritatis, quantum debent.*

20.4 *titulos*   This word refers to inscriptions with the emperor's
name and full titulature. See 19.9 and 11

20.4 *Hadrianopolis*   Eight such foundations are known, the
majority in Asia Minor: in Mysia, Caria, Bithynia, Pisidia,
Cilicia, Lycia, Epirus, and Thrace. Note also Hadrianotherae
(20.13), and numerous others with similar names such as
Hadrianeia and Hadriane.

20.4 *Karthaginem et Athenarum partem*   The author of the HA has
frequent reference to Carthage; was he perhaps African in origin?
See E. Birley (3). No other source records the change of name.
It may be fancy, it may have been connected with the emperor's
visit. But with Athens there is no doubt; an arch divided the
city of Theseus from that of Hadrian. See Travlos 253-57. The
great ornament of the new city was the completed temple of
Olympian Zeus (see 13.6).

20.5 *aquarum ductus*   We know of those at Athens, Corinth, Antioch, Dyrrhachium, and Sarmizegethusa. There were undoubtedly
others. Dio LXIX 5.3 speaks of his gift of a water supply to
some cities.

20.6 *fisci advocatum*   Whatever the term *fiscus* originally
meant, by the second century it referred most particularly to
the revenues accruing to the emperor from the imperial provinces
and from imperial holdings in senatorial provinces. At the
beginning of his reign, Hadrian had cancelled the enormous

outstanding debt to the *fiscus*, which had proved uncollectable (see 7.6). But evidently, in the hope that a similar circumstance might not arise in the future, he appointed an *advocatus fisci* to represent the treasury in dealings with private persons. There was now, so to speak, an official state prosecutor whose charge it was to collect the monies due.

20.7 *orationes* A little is known of Hadrian's oratorical achievement, although fragmentary and random. Charisius the grammarian reports that there was a collection of at least twelve books of Hadrian's speeches; it would seem likely that each book contained more than one speech. From book I is cited Hadrian's doubt whether the word *obiter* is Latin (271.20 Barwick) and from the twelfth book the use of the word *valdissime* (287.1). Two speeches are preserved in part, a third reported in indirect discourse. The former are his allocutions to the African army (Smallwood 328) and his laudation of his mother-in-law Matidia (Smallwood 114; see 9.9 and 19.5); the latter is his reply when the inhabitants of his patria, Italica, requested change of status from a *municipium* to a *colonia*: *De cuius opinionis tam promiscae erroribus divus Hadrianus in oratione, quam de* Italicensibus, *unde ipse ortus fuit, in senatu habuit, peritissime disseruit mirarique se ostendit, quod et ipsi Italicenses et quaedam item alia municipia antiqua, in quibus Uticenses nominat, cum suis moribus legibusque uti possent, in ius coloniarum mutari gestiverint* (Gellius XVI 13.4). A quotation which may derive from a speech is preserved in the life of Avidius Cassius (see 20.3). Three letters may perhaps be mentioned in this context, because they are rather substantial in length and give an opportunity to judge his style: the letter to Servianus about Egypt, if not bogus (*Quadr. Tyr.* 8.1-10, on which see Syme [11] chap. 2), his exchange with Plotina about the succession of the school of Epicurus (Smallwood 442), and his rescript to Minicius Fundanus on the Christians (Freudenberger 218).

For more, in general, see Alexander and Hänel.

*Ipse* is crucial in this sentence. Hadrian, as *quaestor Augusti*, had read out Trajan's speeches (3.11). However widespread the practice was for the emperor to reply personally to petitions, clearly our author or his source assumed that the emperor normally left that task to subordinates. See Millar 240ff.

20.8 *dicaculus* The witticism immediately following is paralleled by an epigram of Ausonius, *De Myrone qui Laidis noctem rogaverat* (XXXVIII [XVII], Peiper p. 326). Some scholars assume that the author of the HA borrowed it from Ausonius, and thus claim a *terminus post quem* for composition; Ausonius died about 395. But of course that need not be; the jest could have been a commonplace, for which it would be vain to seek a source.

20.8 *infecto* From *inficio*, 'dye,' not the negation of *facio*, 'undone.'

20.9 *nomenclatore* The *nomenclator* was a slave whose task it was to remember the names of his master's clients, dependents, and other acquaintances inferior in rank to him. For some persons he served a useful purpose, those who had an enormous number of acquaintances, but many were too stupid or lazy to keep, or bother to keep, names straight.

20.10 *veteranorum nomina* See 10.8, 17.6

20.11 *uno tempore* Hadrian's ability to perform all four activities simultaneously may be subject to doubt, but it need not be rejected out of hand. Later on, Marcus, while attending circus performances, *legeret audiretque ac suscriberet*, and gained unpopularity therefrom (*MA* 15.1). Julius Caesar, similarly, had attended to much public business while at the games, and had offended the populace thereby; Augustus, with his accustomed shrewdness and feeling for public opinion, had abstained from this practice and had shown interest in the performances--indeed, he probably enjoyed them (Suet. *Aug.* 45.1).

20.12 *equos et canes* The text of the verse tribute that Hadrian paid his favorite horse Borysthenes, inscribed on its tombstone, has survived (Smallwood 520):

> *Borysthenes Alanus*
> *Caesareus Veredus,*
> *per aequor et paludes*
> *et tumulos Etruscos*
> *volare qui solebat*
> *Pannonicos in apros,*
> *nec ullus insequentem*
> *dente aper albicanti*
> *ausus fuit nocere*
> *vel extimam salivam*

> *sparsit ab ore caudam,*
> *ut solet evenire;*
> *sed integer iuventa*
> *inviolatus artus*
> *die sua peremptus*
> *hoc situs est in agro.*

See also Dio LXIX 10.2.

20.13 *Hadrianotheras*  In Mysia, a province of Asia Minor. The year was 123.

20.13 *ursam*  Hadrian must have killed bears on more than one occasion and in more than one place. There is preserved an epigram which he wrote when he presented a bearskin to the temple of Eros at Thespiae (*IG* VII 1828). A poem by Pancrates, celebrating a lion hunt by Hadrian and Antinous, partially survives on a papyrus (*P. Oxy.* 1085); Dio LXIX 10.3$^2$ speaks of Hadrian slaying a boar.

The bear hunt which led to the founding of Hadrianotherae took place in 123, that in Thespiae in 125, and the lion hunt in Libya in 130. The plot of the four consulars (see 7.1-2) was evidenced in part, according to Dio LXIX 2.5, during a hunt, while our author speaks of it when Hadrian was sacrificing. The differing circumstances are compatible if we assume that a sacrifice followed the hunt. For Hadrian's hunting in general, see Aymard 173-82, 523-37.

21.1 *iudicis*  For *iudiciis*. See 18.1

21.1 *quamdiu*  This word is used in the sense of "until" to introduce a temporal purpose clause under the influence of *dum*. In this sense, it is first found in the jurists of the second century, and is popular in late Latin.

21.2 *libertos*  The influence of freedmen at the highest levels of government is one of the commonplaces of early imperial history, with its chief locus the principate of Claudius. Pliny invokes this theme among his many points of praise of Trajan (*Pan.* 88.1-2): *Plerique principes, cum essent civium domini, libertorum erant servi: horum consiliis, horum nutu regebantur, per hos audiebant, per hos loquebantur; per hos praeturae et sacerdotia et consulatus, immo ab his petebantur. tu libertis tuis summum quidem honorem, sed tamquam libertis habes abundeque sufficere his credis, si probi et frugi existimentur. scis enim praecipuum esse indicium non magni principis magnos libertos.*

If Pliny is correct, then the stricture of our author that Hadrian faulted all his predecessors cannot stand. For Hadrian's use of *equites* rather than *liberti*, see 22.8 (although not fully accurate).

For the anecdote about the slave walking between two senators, cf. Suetonius' comment about Claudius' *a studiis* Polybius (28.2): *qui saepe inter duos consules ambulabat.*

21.3 *e conspectu* "from his presence"

21.4 *tetrafarmacum* This delicacy is elsewhere said to have been the invention of Ceionius Commodus, the later Aelius Caesar, and to have actually been a *pentefarmacum*, the ingredients of which were *sumen, fasianum, pavo, perna crustulata,* and *apruna* (*Ael.* 5.4). But the life of Alexander Severus (30.6) speaks again of the *tetrafarmacum*, with Marius Maximus as the source, whose authority is also invoked in the Aelius life for the smaller number. But it should be noted that the difference between the two recipes is of two ingredients rather than one, since *perna* and *crustulo*, itemized separately here, are combined in the Aelius life as *perna crustulata*. The added ingredients are pheasant and boar; perhaps Commodus was responsible for both dishes. Cazzaniga 365 proposes to emend: *de fasiano, sumine, perna [et] crustula ⟨ta⟩⟨et apruna.⟩* Apruna is a kind of meat. He also insists upon the spelling *pentafarmacum*, not *pentefarmacum*.

21.5-6 *fames, pestilentia, terrae motus, Tiberis inundatio* All these natural occurrences were considered ill omens; they were classed as *adversa*.

21.7 *Latium* This refers to the *ius Latii*, the right of citizens of Latin communities, in the early republic, to gain Roman citizenship by taking up residence in Rome. In the second century B.C., when the movement of individuals threatened to depopulate the individual communities, this right was limited to the magistrates of the communities, and became known as *ius civitatis per honorem adipiscendae*. With the passage of time, this privilege was granted to communities throughout the empire, so that its local connection, first with Latium, then with Italy, disappeared. Hadrian established a new aspect of this privilege, known as *Latium maius*, whereby not only the local magistrates but also the city councilors, the *decuriones*, gained Roman citizenship.

21.7 *tributa*  See 21.12

21.8 *Expeditiones . . . bella*  Hadrian indeed undertook no wars on his own initiative, and the armies, although kept in strict training, were frequently employed in large building programs, such as the wall across the north of Britain. But there were two major wars to which he had to respond, the great uprising of the Jews, which was fought out with the greatest bitterness and severity on both sides, from 132 to 135, and one begun by the Alani, about 134, which was brought to an end by gifts and the threat of force posed by Flavius Arrianus, the governor of Cappadocia. The Romans suffered such terrible losses against the Jews that Hadrian, reporting victory to the senate, did not use the customary salutation (Dio LXIX 14.3), "If you and your children are in health, it is well; I and the legions are in health."

21.9 *curam exercitus nimiam*  Respect, not affection, is the emotion one anticipates toward him from the army, because he was a hard taskmaster, who insisted upon stern discipline in peace as in war. He shared their privations and discomforts, and encouraged their allegiance by *praemiis* and *honoribus* (10.2); that these were the basis of the adjective *liberalissimus* is likely. He did not increase the soldiers' pay. See the whole of chapter 10.

21.10 *regem*  See 5.4. For this whole section, see 17.10ff. It seems out of place, recapitulating material given earlier, and moving from comments favorable to Hadrian to those tending to ridicule.

21.11 *Armeniis regem*  This was Vologaesus. The Roman legate, the first and only one, was L. Catilius Severus (see 5.10).

21.12 *tributum*  The text suggests that Hadrian retained the power to impose tribute, but chose not to use it.

21.13 *Albanos et Hiberos*  The Albani lived along the coast of the Caspian Sea, south of the Caucasus. The Hiberi were their western neighbors.

21.13 *contempsissent* See 13.9

21.14 *Bactranorum* Bactria was an enormous territory east of the Parthian domain, corresponding in part to modern Afghanistan.

22.1 *Tutores* The important thing in the guardianship of a minor or a female who was without the supervision of a *paterfamilias* was not moral guidance but the maintenance of the integrity of property. Until age seven, a child could not act for himself at all; thereafter, he could enter into valid legal arrangements with the approval of his *tutor*; by giving or withholding this approval (*auctoritas*), the latter was able to control the actions of his ward. One or more tutors could be designated in a will or appointed by a magistrate; they could act jointly or designate one of their number to carry out, on behalf of all, their obligations; he was called the *tutor gerens*. See Kaser 352-69.

Hadrian largely eliminated the *tutela mulierum* by permitting women to make wills on their own. He himself had had two *tutores*, Trajan and Attianus, who seem to have taken much more concern for him than merely preservation of his property (see 1.4-2.2). His own experience may well have influenced his concern in this branch of law.

22.1 *disciplinam* Examples of his concern for "civilian" life, in a rather conservative vein, with measures harking back to precedents of Augustus and Tiberius, follow in sections 2-7. For *disciplina militaris*, see 3.9 and the whole of 10. For the word *civilem* in a wider sense, see 20.1.

22.2 *togatos* The toga, the article of clothing that differentiated the Roman citizen from all other peoples, was a heavy, warm, and cumbersome garment, worn only when necessary on public and formal occasions even in the late republic and early principate. Suet. *Aug.* 40.5 reports Augustus' outrage at the neglect of the toga: *Etiam habitum vestitumque pristinum reducere studuit, ac visa quondam pro contione pullatorum turba indignabundus et clamitans: en*

*Romanos rerum dominos, gentemque togatam*
(Vergil *Aen.* I 282) *negotium aedilibus dedit, ne quem posthac paterentur in foro circove nisi positis lacernis togatum consistere.*

The word *pristinus* suits Hadrian's taste in general (see 16.5).

22.4 *stans* An action displaying his *civilitas* (see 20.1). Caesar had earned great unpopularity by remaining seated to

Commentary 127

receive senators (Suet. *Jul.* 78.1): *Verum praecipuam et exitiabilem sibi invidiam hinc maxime movit. adeuntis se cum plurimis honorificentissimisque decretis universos patres conscriptos sedens pro aede Veneris Genetricis excepit.* Granted that that had been a public occasion in a public place, nonetheless Hadrian here comported himself as host rather than as princeps. See 9.7-8

22.4 *pallio* The *pallium* was a rectangular mantle, lighter, more easily donned, and more comfortable, than the toga. It was known among the Greeks as the *himation*, and in the empire was recognized as the garb peculiar to philosophers.

22.4 *toga summissa* "with his toga hanging loosely"

22.5 *sumptus convivii* What was the *anticus modus* to which Hadrian reduced these expenses? We have no way of knowing.
Sumptuary legislation had been passed by Augustus (Suet. *Aug.* 34.1). It had not been successful. Tiberius, himself *princeps antiquae parsimoniae* (Tac. *Ann.* III 52.1), argued against further legislation, since it would be fruitless (*Ann.* III 53-5). For his own actions to limit extravagance, including the use of food from the day before and half-eaten on holidays, see Suet. *Tib.* 34.1.
In his actions toward his subjects, Hadrian was only following the practice which he pursued himself (see 9.8).

22.6 *vehicula* Caesar had been responsible for a law which, with only a few exceptions, had forbidden wheeled traffic in Rome during the day. The details are preserved in the *lex Iulia municipalis* (*FIRA* I 13, lines 56-61): *Quae viae in urbe Roma sunt erunt intra ea loca, ubi continenti habitabitur, ne quis in ieis vieis post k. Ianuar. primas plostrum interdiu post solem ortum, neve ante horam X diei ducito agito, nisi quod aedium sacrarum deorum immortalium caussa aedificandarum, operisve publice faciumdei causa advehei portari oportebit, aut quod ex urbe exve ieis loceis earum rerum, quae publice demoliendae locatae erunt, publice exportarei oportebit, et quarum rerum caussa plostra h. l. certeis hominibus certeis de causeis agere ducere licebit.*
These prohibitions remained in effect in the principate. Claudius extended them to the towns of Italy (Suet. *Claud.* 25.2). This passage tells us that Hadrian limited the loads that could

be brought into the city. Marcus (*MA* 23.8) forbade wheeled
traffic in every community of the empire.

Nonetheless, chaos reigned at night, making life unpleasant
for the poor and sleep almost impossible. Juvenal is the chief
witness (*Sat.* III 236-59).

22.6 *equos* Hadrian's prohibition of horseback riding in cities
seems not to have been effectual, since Marcus (*MA* 23.8) was
compelled to prohibit the same thing, unless this latter statement is an unhistorical doublet.

22.7 *ante octavam horam* Juvenal (*Sat.* XI 205) tells us that
the baths opened at the fifth hour, Martial (*Ep.* X 48.3) speaks
of the sixth. Both agree that the opening was before noon. Since
the length of the hour varied with the season, varying between
a maximum of seventy-seven minutes and a minimum of forty-three,
the fifth hour would come at about 9:25 at the summer solstice
and at about 10:35 at the winter solstice. Hadrian's prohibition
of the use of the public baths before early afternoon will have
stretched out the working day by several hours and will also,
perhaps, have made the baths available longer for women, in
those establishments which did not have separate facilities. See
18.11

22.8 *ab epistolis et a libellis* These secretaryships, concerned
respectively with imperial correspondence and petitions, along
with others, of which the most important was the *a rationibus*,
whose province was finance, were filled first by freedmen of the
emperor. Augustus found it necessary to invoke the assistance of
both freedmen and slaves from his household to carry on the
enormous tasks of administration of the empire, and did not feel
it proper or appropriate to ask men of free birth to undertake
such responsibilities. The freedmen who held these influential
posts waxed most prominent under Claudius. But in the turmoil
of 69, *equites* performed some of these duties under both Otho
and Vitellius, and Domitian was the first, without the pressure
of war and its attendant abnormality, to assign these posts to
both *equites* and freedmen (Suet. *Dom.* 7.2). Thus the author's
statement about Hadrian being *primus* is false. See Smallwood
270; Millar 83-101.

22.9 *ditavit* See 15.1, 17.6

22.10 *sacra Romana diligentissime curavit, peregrina contempsit*
In this he partially followed the precedent of Augustus (Suet. *Aug.* 93), but, nonetheless, his view of what was Roman was wider than that of the first emperor. "For the first time a Roman emperor is represented with his foot resting on a crocodile. This means that the emperor is an incarnation of Horus. . . . It is the most extreme form of divine honour known to the Romans.

"The attitude of the emperor towards Egypt was a curious one. From the beginning of his reign he had great interest in his Egyptian private domain. He was the first to have the images of Isis and Serapis on his coins. The Alexandrian gods are regarded as Roman gods. . . ." The statement here given in the *Vita* "implies in the case of the Egyptian cults that they were treated as Roman, for the emperor took great care of the Egyptian cults and sanctuaries." (den Boer [1] 140-41)

Sestertii and dupondii of the latter part of Hadrian's reign depict him standing with his foot on a crocodile. As Horus, he is king of Egypt. These coins were not issued before 134, perhaps in connection with the building of a cenotaph in honor of Antinous in Rome. This is recorded on an obelisk, which was perhaps part of the decoration, and which survives, now located on the Pincio. See Levi.

22.11 *pontificis maximi officium* Every emperor from Augustus on into the fourth century was *pontifex maximus*, so that this notice occasions some surprise. It may give a hint of the date of composition of the *Vita*, for Gratian was the first emperor to refuse the office, about 375. In such circumstances, when the emperor was Christian and divested himself of any pagan traces, a reader might well require elucidation on something which had earlier been routine.

Augustus had to wait until 12 B.C. to become chief pontiff, because Lepidus lived on in his comfortable retirement until that year and Augustus refused to strip him of the office.

22.11 *causas*  See 8.9

22.11 *consilio*  See 18.1

22.12 *Fucinum lacum*  The Fucine lake, located in the center of Italy, almost due east of Rome, in the land of the Marsi, was subject to overflowing. Hence Caesar planned to drain it, but he did not live to undertake the task. Claudius accomplished it with great difficulty and expense over a period of eleven years; an *emissarium* of some 3 1/2 miles was dug. This enormous engineering project was not fully successful, for it required the attention of both Trajan (Smallwood 388) and Hadrian to keep the *emissarium* under repair.

22.13 *quattuor consulares*  Prior to this innovation, legal jurisdiction throughout Italy had been in the hands of the praetors. The necessity for all litigants to come to Rome caused inconvenience or hardship to those involved and evidently overwhelmed the praetors. With the appointment of four men of consular rank who would go on circuit throughout the regions assigned them, the benefit of law was more easily brought to the residents of Italy and the jurisdiction of the praetor was now limited to the city of Rome and a radius of one hundred miles from the capital. Whether this rather revolutionary change was popular cannot be determined, although it seems not to have been, for Antoninus discontinued it (Appian *B.C.* I 38). Under it, jurisdiction in Italy was like that in the provinces, and the Italians may have resented such a seeming diminution in their status.

Antoninus had personal experience of the reform (*AP* 2.11). Whatever his reasons for not continuing the practice, Marcus reinstated it on the basis of Hadrian's precedent (*MA* 11.6).

Their judicial powers were limited to civil cases; criminal cases were the responsibility of the *praefectus praetorio* or the *praefectus urbis*.

22.14 *pluit*  Cf. 25.1-4

23.1 *peragratis*  See 17.8

23.1 *capite nudo*  See 17.9

23.1 *morbum lectualem*  Dio LXIX 20.1 says that he first became consumptive and then suffered from dropsy.

23.2 *Serviano*  The same statement, with similarity of language, occurs in 15.8, 23.8, and 25.8. See the comment on the first.

23.3 *Fuscum*  H. Peter's text read ⟨*item*⟩ *Fuscum, quod imperium* etc., thereby linking Servianus and his grandson, who, Dio LXIX 2.6, 17.1 tells us, were put to death together. A Greek horoscope is linked with Fuscus; he is thus shown to be not eighteen years old but in his twenty-fourth year at the time of his death (year of birth 113, not 118), to have had distinguished

# Commentary 131

ancestry, with his father, Cn. Pedanius Fuscus Salinator, the emperor's colleague in the ordinary consulship of 118, and to have been involved in a plot, and thus charged with *maiestas*, led on by his belief in *praesagia et ostenta*. It appears that he was groomed to be Hadrian's successor from an early age, with marked signs of favor, but, as Hadrian's ill health became more critical, was found to be inadequate and was passed over for Ceionius Commodus. Hence his fatal attempt to salvage his position. Therefore it seems that it was Fuscus who was responsible for his grandfather's downfall, and not the reverse. For full discussion, see Champlin; for Hadrian's interest and skill in astrology, see 2.4 and 16.7.

23.4 *Platorium Nepotem* See 4.2

23.5 *Terentium Gentianum* The author errs, for Gentianus had been dead for some years. D. Terentius Gentianus was one of Trajan's marshals, a bit of a prodigy, reaching the consulship, as suffect in 116, before the age of thirty. But Hadrian never put him in command of a province; it may be that he considered him too much of a rival. His sister commemorated him in an epitaph inscribed on a pyramid while she was visiting Egypt (perhaps in Hadrian's company, in 130):

> *Vidi pyramidas sine te, dulcissime frater,*
> *et tibi, quod potui, lacrimas hic moesta profudi,*
> *et nostri memorem luctus hanc sculpo querelam.*
> *Sit nomen Decimi Gentian{n}i pyramide alta,*
> *pontificis comitisque tuis, Traiane, triumphis,*
> *lustra \<que\> sex intra censoris, consulis, esse*
>
> _____     (Smallwood 237)

23.7 *crudelitatis . . . repressit* Cf. Tacitus' character sketch of Tiberius (*Ann.* VI 51.3): *intestabilis saevitia, sed obtectis libidinibus, dum Seianum dilexit timuitve.*

23.7 *villa Tiburtina* See 26.5

23.8 *Servianum* More detail is offered here for Hadrian's enmity than in the comparable notices at 15.8, 23.2, and 25.8. For the omens and their importance, see 2.4.

Dio LXIX 17.2 reports that, before his execution, Servianus "asked for fire, and as he offered incense he exclaimed: 'That I am guilty of no wrong, ye, O Gods, are well aware; as for Hadrian, this is my only prayer, that he may long for death but be unable to die.'" And that indeed is what occurred.

23.8 *multis aliis* There is no evidence for anyone other than Servianus and Fuscus being put to death in the last years of Hadrian's reign (see 11.3). The exaggeration probably stems from senatorial enmity, which sought to put a similar blot on this period as the affair of the four consulars had done at the beginning. Yet Antoninus was called Pius, in one version, *quod multos senatores Hadriano iam saevienti abripuisset* (24.4); similarly, *ob leves offensas plurimos iussit occidi, quos Antoninus reservavit* (25.8).

23.9 *Sabina uxor* The marriage, which occurred in the year 100, was not a happy one. Hadrian found her tedious, and would have divorced her had his public position not deterred him (11.3). Nonetheless, his relationship with her was at least outwardly correct, as exemplified by his discharge of the praetorian prefect and the *ab epistulis* for lack of respect toward her. Sabina accompanied Hadrian on many of his travels, but it does not seem likely that she was with him on all.

Sabina did not bear any children; whether because barren or because of precautions that she had taken is by no means clear. *Epit.* 14.8 reports the latter: *Quae palam iactabat se, quod immane ingenium probavisset, elaborasse, ne ex eo ad humani generis perniciem gravidaretur.*

She received the title Augusta about the year 128 and was honored on coins. She died in 136, with gossip suggesting either foul play or suicide (*Epit.* 14.8: *dum prope servilibus iniuriis afficitur, ad mortem voluntariam compulsa*). Neither report need be believed. Upon her death, she was deified, and she is among the *divae* honored in the *feriale Duranum*. She was further honored by reliefs on an arch built by Hadrian, now known as the Arco di Portogallo, with one relief representing her apotheosis, another depicting Hadrian delivering the address over his departed wife. Her appearance is well known, from coins, reliefs, and statues. See Carandini and Nash 86. See also 1.2, 9.9.

23.10 *Ceionium Commodum* There has been much speculation and debate about Hadrian's plan for the succession. L. Ceionius Commodus was *cos. ord.* when adopted in 136; his family embraced numerous consulars, and it may have been this nobility which attracted Hadrian. "Around Ceionius was massed an influential group that took its origin in three marriages a generation earlier of a lady called Plautia (her name emerges from genealogical reconstruction). She was the wife in succession of Ceionius Commodus (*cos*.106), Avidius Nigrinus (*suff*. 110), Vettulenus Cerialis (*cos*. 106)." (Syme [10] 93)  Yet there were shortcomings which made the choice less than wise: his health was bad, though this was obviously not a major factor at the time of adoption, and he was in no way a *vir militaris*, having had an exclusively civilian career. It is doubtful that Hadrian was moved by the unjustified (?) death of Nigrinus in the affair of the four consulars (7.1-2) to honor his step-son and subsequent son-in-law. Some scholars claim that Ceionius was Hadrian's bastard son; that need not be believed. Did he have any special qualities which would have suggested him as a worthy princeps?

It would not appear so. In this passage, the only recommendation is *forma*, which is reproduced in the life of *Ael*. 5.1, *Hadriano, ut malevoli loquuntur, acceptior forma quam moribus*. His life was frivolous, his tastes luxurious, his abilities such that he scarcely seemed *capax imperii*. Was Hadrian just wrong, or did he hope to gain the support of a powerful faction in the senate, or in despair of his illness, and fearing a sudden death, did he just choose one who was very near to hand, one of the consuls? We shall never know, although such a choice appears as an aberration of judgment. See, inter alia, Pflaum (2) and Barnes (1).

23.11 *Verum* This is an error; he was never called Verus. This stems from confusion with his son, who, however, was not called Verus until after he became joint Augustus in 161, when Marcus ordered that he be called by his own (i.e. Marcus') name.

23.11 *Aelium* He became an Aelius by adoption into Hadrian's family.

23.12 *donativum* See 5.7

23.13 *praetura* Not so; he had held the praetorship in 130 and was consul when selected. See 23.10

23.13 *Pannoniis* The two Pannonias, superior and inferior, constituted a major command. Nearest of all the Danube provinces to the heartland of Italy, their security and defense were essential for the well-being of the empire. From Pannonia had come the decisive thrust in the civil war of 69, under impetus of Antonius Primus, and Septimius Severus was to claim the principate from Pannonia in 193. Hadrian's intent was probably to display his intended heir to the armies and accustom him to the demands of provincial administration. Nor did Commodus, now L. Aelius Caesar, fall short of the task: *nec provinciae quidem, cui praepositus erat, defuit. nam bene gestis rebus vel potius feliciter etiamsi non summi, medii tamen optinuit ducis famam* (*Ael*.3.5-6). The judgment is not dissimilar to Tacitus' on Otho, whose effective government of Lusitania occasioned surprise (*Ann*. XII 46.3).

23.13 *secundo consulem* This was for 137; both his consulates were ordinary.

23.14 *minus sanum* For further discussion of Hadrian's response to his illness, see *Ael*. 3.7-4.8, 6.1-5, where the amount of money distributed is given as 300,000,000 sesterces.

23.16 *Votorum causa* On the first day of each year, public vows were offered for the well-being of the state and the oath of allegiance to the emperor was renewed. For this formal ceremony to be interrupted by public mourning would have rendered its purposes invalid.

24.1 *Arrium Antoninum* His full name is T. Aurelius Fulvius Boionius Arrius Antoninus. Previous generations contained numerous consuls; born in 86, he reached the consulate in 120, at an early age. Soon thereafter, he was appointed one of the four *consulares* to whom jurisdiction of Italy was assigned (see 22.13) and was proconsul of Asia about 134/35. One of the most distinguished men of his time, and a close associate of Hadrian, although exclusively experienced in civilian enterprises, he was a far sounder choice than Ceionius Commodus had been.

24.1 *Pius* In addition to the three alternative reasons given below (24.3-4) for this honorific *cognomen*, the life of Antoninus offers two more (2.6-7): *vel quod, cum se Hadrianus interimere vellet, ingenti custodia et diligentia fecit, ne id posset admittere, vel quod vere natura clementissimus et nihil temporibus suis asperum fecit*. The most likely reason is his gaining of deification for Hadrian against the inclinations of the senate (see Eutr. VIII 7.3).

24.1 *Annium Verum et Marcum Antoninum* The former is the son of Commodus, now seven years old, whose name remained L. Ceionius

Commodus even after the adoption of his father as Caesar, who
was now known as Lucius Aelius Aurelius Commodus. Annius Verus
is wrongly given. The latter was indeed named M. Annius Verus;
now seventeen years old, he had been much honored by Hadrian,
who jokingly used to call him Verissimus. His name was now
Marcus Aelius Aurelius Verus. After Hadrian's death, he married
Antoninus' daughter Annia Galeria Faustina.

The two young men succeeded Antoninus as joint Augusti in
161, the former as Imp. Caesar L. Aurelius Verus Augustus, the
latter as Imp. Caesar M. Aurelius Antoninus Augustus; Verus
died in 167, and Marcus reigned alone until 180, although his
son Commodus had the title *Augustus* from late November 176.

24.6 *Catilius Severus*   See 5.10

24.9 *in . . . usque*   *Usque* seems superfluous; *usque ad* to express "place to which" is common, as is *usque* alone. But with *in* it serves only for emphasis.

24.10 *dicente Antonino*   This entire absolute appears to be misplaced. Its present position destroys the continuity of thought. It fits much more suitably following *morbi ferret* three lines earlier, so that there will be a sequence of three ablative participles, with a crescendo of emotion and personality.

24.11 *iterum*   Hadrian's vain attempts to end his life fulfilled Servianus' prayer (see 23.8).

25.1-4 *ea tempestate*   These miracles focus upon the general belief that the emperor is all-powerful and can alter the course of nature. Similar is the episode of rain after extended drought (22.14). Vespasian's exploits in Alexandria may be compared (Tac. *Hist.* IV 81).

25.4 *Marius Maximus*   See 2.10

25.5 *Baias*   There was at least one imperial villa at Baiae; the Aragonese castle of Don Pedro, which stands now at the southern extremity of Baiae on the road to Bacoli (the ancient Bauli), is generally thought to have been built on its foundations. Burial in Cicero's villa at Puteoli, which was quite near, was at best a temporary expedient (if it occurred at all), for elsewhere we are told that Antoninus took the remains to Rome and buried them in the gardens of Domitia (*AP* 5.1, *MA* 6.1). This too was only temporary, for in the following year Hadrian was

buried in the great mausoleum that he had begun a few years
before, but which was not yet finished when he died. Sabina's
ashes were transported there as well (Smallwood 124). For the
Mausoleum, see 19.11.

25.7 *invisusque omnibus*  See 23.8

25.8 *Servianum . . . ut supra dictum est*  See 15.8, 23.2, and
23.8

25.9 *hos versus*  The authenticity of these verses has long been
subject to doubt, most recently, with recapitulation of earlier
argument, by Barnes (2). Convincing refutation is offered by
Baldwin (1), on the basis of language and tone, with little
emphasis placed upon external argument. This, I think, is the
right approach, for not everything that the HA offers in point of
detail is false or bogus; we know independently (Dio LXIX 3.1)
that Hadrian composed both prose and verse.

Similar debate has occurred over the adjectives in line
four: are they to be construed with *animula* (1) or *loca* (3), or,
indeed, are they to be divided between the two nouns? It seems
best to construe them with *animula*; lines one and four are almost
precisely the same metrically, and all the liquid diminutives
combine to emphasize the fragility of the little soul. This is
also the view of Mayer, who, however, punctuates with an interro-
gation at the end, since line 3 is a question and *nec dabis* is
no more than *non datura*. I find this unconvincing.

Mariotti assigns the adjectives to *loca*. Gallavotti accepts
Mariotti's text but argues that *pallidula nudula* refer to
*animula blandula, rigida* to *loca*. Their third line reads
    *quo nunc abibis? In loca*

25.10 *tales*  Other than the lines above and the exchange with
Florus (see 16.4), Morel, *FPL* 136, offers only one additional
line, in honor of his deceased poet friend, Voconius:
    *lascivus versu, mente pudicus eras.*
This has reminiscence of Ovid and Martial. See also 20.12

25.10 *Graecos*  Four brief poems are preserved under his name
in the Greek anthology: 6,332 (see 14.3), 7,674, 9,17 and 387.
The authorship of the last two is disputable; they are also
assigned to Germanicus Caesar. Bühler publishes a three line
epigram attributed to Hadrian, but denies the authorship. See
also Dio LXIX 11.1 (see 14.4).

25.11 *vixit* Dio LXIX 23.1 reports that his life was two days longer than is indicated here. That is an error. Hadrian was born January 24 and died July 10. The *dies imperii* which he celebrated was August 11. The precision of the figures depends upon inclusive reckoning.

26.1 *promissa barba* Beards had been commonplace in the early and mid republic. The second century B.C. saw the general triumph of shaving, and throughout the next two hundred and more years beards were quite uncommon, only affected by men such as Clodius and his friends (Cicero speaks of the *barbula*). Gaius (Suet. *Cal.* 52) frequently appeared with a golden beard, but that may have been merely for show. Nero, perhaps because of his artistic pretensions, had a modest beard, but he is the only emperor so depicted before Hadrian. Perhaps his reason was as given here; it may be, however, that he chose thereby to show himself in the line of Greek philosophers.

26.2 *armis* See 14.10

26.3 *venatus* See 2.1, 20.13

26.4 *Attellanas* The *fabula Atellana* was one of the antecedents of Roman comedy. A rustic farce with stock characters, which originated in Atella, near Capua, in Oscan country, it was another instance of Hadrian's delight in, and preference for, archaic literature (see 16.6).

26.4 *sambucas* The *sambuca* was a Greek musical instrument, like a harp, triangular in shape.

26.4 *pro re* "according to circumstances"

26.5 *Tiburtinam villam* To speak of Hadrian's enormous complex as a villa is misleading, for the tendency is to think of one main building with a number of outbuildings. This is rather an estate, covering some 700 acres, embracing numbers of different complexes of buildings, almost all built in some axial relationship with one or more others. The site is on the lowlands to the west of the slopes of Tibur, the modern Tivoli, some thirty kilometers east of Rome. Hadrian began construction on this complex early in his reign, and the scope grew as his travels revealed more of the wonders of the civilized world to him (see 17.8). Several of the major buildings have in recent years been restored; the names given them and others are uncertain, their source being this passage. See W. L. MacDonald, s.v. Tibur, *The Princeton Encyclopedia of Classical Sites* (Princeton 1976) 921-2, Kähler, and Aurigemma. For Hadrian's other building activity, see 19.9-13.

26.6 *signa mortis* These can better be called *omina mortis*. The author has given six, artistically arranged in three pairs. The first pair, with the *praetexta* and the *anulus*, occurred on Hadrian's birthday. Yet the first item is suspect; the chief event clearly was the *commendatio* of Antoninus, in connection with which Hadrian was performing a sacrifice, with the fold of his toga over his head. Yet earlier Hadrian was said to be ill, indeed gravely ill, when he adopted him (23.1, 24.1, 24.8). The first passage states that he was confined to his bed; Dio LXIX 20.1-5 reports this as well, having Hadrian commend his successor while bedridden. Under such circumstances, Hadrian could hardly have been involved in a religious ceremony. The slipping of his ring from his finger is more meaningful, for the transmission of a ring was recognized as one of the aspects of a change of rule. Indeed, Hadrian's own ambition had been whetted by the gift of a ring, given by Nerva to Trajan and by him to Hadrian (3.7). Could this have been the same ring?

The next pair of events occurred before the emperor's birthday, and both in the senate. The unintelligible gibberish of the unknown man was in itself ominous; *ululans* suggests the howling of animals. Was Hadrian so upset because he knew his end was near? He was skilled in astrology, and (we are told) was able to forecast all the events up to the close of his life (16.7). His misspeaking his own death rather than that of his first successor was indeed a prodigy.

So too were the dreams, since they frequently served as a preview. Since Hadrian was an enthusiastic and skilled hunter, the second dream clearly forecast death, when in the past he had so frequently slain animals. See 2.1, 20.13, 26.3

See Mouchová (1) 112-15.

26.6 *Antoninum commendaret* Although Hadrian designated Antoninus his heir on January 24, the latter was not actually adopted until late February (*AP* 4.6).

27.1 *In mortuum* There is no doubt of his unpopularity at his death, though the reasons for it must remain obscure, if one rejects the tradition of a real or intended bloodbath of senators. For the ambivalent feelings of Fronto toward Hadrian, for whom he had respect but not affection, see his letter to Marcus (II 1.1; Haines I 110-11): *Hadrianum . . . propitium et placatum magis volui quam amavi.* See 25.7

27.1 *inrita* This would have been the consequence had the senate voted *damnatio memoriae* against him, which would have entailed destruction of all statues and images of him, erasure of his name and titles from all inscriptions, and invalidation of all his actions (*rescissio actorum*). Such a step had been taken against Domitian, and was later to be taken against Commodus and Elagabalus. *Damnatio memoriae* was a much stronger judgment on the senate's part of an emperor's rule than refusal to designate him a *divus*.

27.2 *divus* By voting for deification of a deceased princeps, the senate indicated its belief that he had ruled "constitutionally," which largely meant that he had respected the prerogatives of the senatorial order. Of Hadrian's predecessors, Tiberius, Gaius, Nero, Galba, Otho, Vitellius, and Domitian had failed of divinization.

27.3 *templum* If such a temple did indeed exist at Puteoli, no trace of it has been so far discovered. But our author fails to mention here the substantial temple built in Hadrian's honor in the early 140s at Rome, now called the Hadrianeum, though it is mentioned in *AP* 8.2. Part of the podium and most of one flank of columns survive, incorporated into the borsa, the stock exchange, of Rome, in the Piazza di Pietra. The chief interest in the temple for modern scholars is the series of reliefs representing the provinces of the empire which decorated the podium. See Nash 457-61.

27.3 *quinquennale certamen et flamines et sodales* There is no other evidence for the establishment of the *certamen* in honor of the deceased emperor. The only precedents in Rome for such an event at five year intervals were the *ludicrum ad morem Graeci certaminis* (Tac. Ann. XIV 20.1) established by Nero and called the *Neronia*, with particular emphasis upon music, poetry, and rhetoric, and the *agon Capitolinus* of Domitian. The *certamen* for *divus Hadrianus* may well have had the same pattern as Nero's, with the addition of equestrian sport and hunting skills. But this must remain conjectural.

The existence of the *flamen*, a priest in the service of an individual god, went back to the days of Numa. During the republic, there were three *flamines maiores*, the *Dialis* who served Jupiter, the *Martialis* who served Mars, and the *Quirinalis* who served Quirinus, and twelve *flamines minores*. Beginning with Julius Caesar, every *divus* up to the third century had his own flamen; Hadrian's was the *flamen Hadrianalis*. He will have presided at religious occasions in honor of Hadrian, such as the sacrifice on his birthday.

*Sodales* were members of minor priesthoods, who could not act as individuals but only as a corporate body. The ancient *sodalitates* were the *Fetiales*, the *Luperci*, the *Salii*, the *Fratres Arvales*, and the *Sodales Titii*. The imperial *sodalitates* had responsibility for the imperial cult, each of emperors linked by family, so that the *sodales Hadrianales* were charged with the cult of Nerva and Trajan as well as that of Hadrian. See Wissowa 342-8, 521-2.

27.4  *Pium*  See 24.1

APPENDIX I

Hadrian's Family

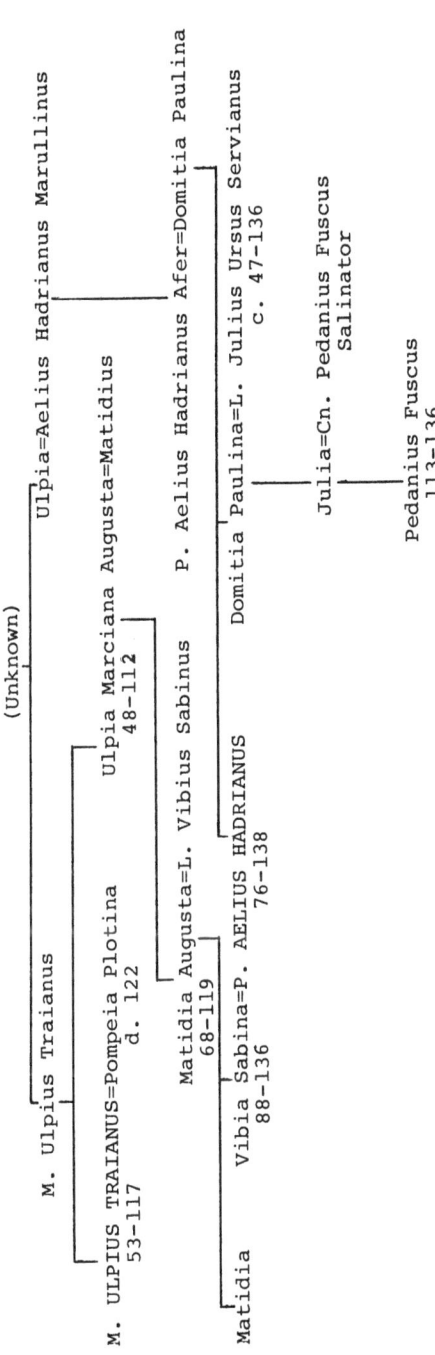

APPENDIX II

Hadrian's career as *privatus*

decemvir stlitibus iudicandis
sevir turmae equitum Romanorum
praefectus urbi feriarum Latinarum
tribunus militum legionis II Adiutricis Piae Fidelis (95)
tribunus militum legionis V Macedonicae (96)
tribunus militum legionis XXII Primigeniae Piae Fidelis (97)
quaestor (101)
ab actis senatus
tribunus plebis (105)
praetor (106)
legatus legionis I Minerviae Piae Fidelis (106)
legatus Augusti pro praetore Pannoniae inferioris (107)
consul suffectus (108)
septemvir epulonum (before 112)
sodalis Augustalis (before 112)
archon Athenis (112/13)
legatus Syriae (117)

The above career is based upon $PIR^2$ and various writings of R. Syme. G. Alföldy, *Die Legionslegaten der römischen Rheinarmeen* (Epigraphische Studien 3, Bonn 1967) 23-24, proposes several major changes, i.e. tribunus plebis 102, praetor 105-106, and legatus of Pannonia inferior 106-108, as well as several smaller, more modest variations.

The Athens Inscription

Smallwood 109. 112, Athens, in the theatre of Dionysus. *ILS*, 308.

P. Aelio P. f. Serg. Hadriano / cos., VII viro epulonum, sodali Augustali, leg. pro pr. imp. Nervae Traiani / Caesaris Aug. Germanici Dacici Pannoniae Inferioris, praetori eodemque / tempore leg. leg. I Minerviae p.f. bello Dacico, item trib. pleb., quaestori imperatoris// Traiani et comiti expeditionis Dacicae, donis militaribus ab eo donato bis, trib. leg. II / Adiutricis p.f. item legionis V Macedonicae item legionis XXII Primigeniae p.f., seviro / turmae eq. R., praef. feriarum Latinarum, X viro s(tlitibus) i(udicandis)
ἡ ἐξ Ἀρείου πάγου βουλὴ καὶ ἡ τῶν ἑξακοσίων καὶ ὁ δῆμος ὁ Ἀθηναίων τὸν ἄρχοντα ἑαυτῶν Ἀδριανόν

APPENDIX III

Hadrian's Titulature

P. *Aelius Hadrianus*; in inscriptions almost always IMP CAESAR TRAIANVS HADRIANVS AVG.

Hadrian received the *tribunicia potestas* on the death of Trajan in August 117, and renewed it on 10 December in the same year, and in all subsequent years.

In the summer of 136 he adopted L. Ceionius Commodus, who took the name of L. Aelius Commodus Verus, and appears in the monuments of 136-137 as L. AELIVS CAESAR. After the death of the latter on 1 Jan. 138, Hadrian adopted T. Aurelius Fulvus Boionius Arrius Antoninus, under the name of T. Aelius Caesar Antoninus, best known as Antoninus Pius.

Antoninus Pius thereupon adopted, as his ultimate joint successors, (1) his nephew, M. Annius Verus, who took the name of M. Aelius Aurelius Verus, best known as Marcus Aurelius, and (2) the son of L. Aelius Caesar above mentioned, named L. Ceionius Commodus, who took the name of L. Aelius Aurelius Commodus, but is best known as Lucius Verus.

| A.D. | | | | |
|---|---|---|---|---|
| 117 | 11 Aug. | IMP·CAES·AVG, PONT·MAX, TR·P | | |
| 118 | 1 Jan. | COS·II (108 COS·I) | | |
| 119 | 1 Jan. | COS·III | | |
| 128 | 21 April | P(ater) P(atriae) | | |
| 135 | | IMP·II | | |
| 136 | 1 Jan. | | Aelius, COS | |
| | | | Aelius CAES, TR·P, PONT | |
| 137 | 1 Jan. | | Aelius COS·II | |
| 138 | 1 Jan. | | Death of Aelius. | |
| | 25 Feb. | | Antoninus, CAES, TR·P, PONT | |
| | 10 July | Death of Hadrian. | | |

from J. E. Sandys, *Latin Epigraphy* (1927[2]), with minor change

APPENDIX IV

The Chronology of Hadrian's Travels

The author of the *Vita Hadriani* speaks of three series of trips outside of Italy; this does not, of course, include the necessary journey from the east to Rome when he first returned to the capital after his accession.

The crucial passage covers 10.1 to 14.5. Not everything included in these pages has to do with his travels, and much has been intruded which would find a more suitable home elsewhere. The author does not divide the trips, nor does he furnish chronological details, and he is selective in the places that he mentions. The three trips are divided as follows:

| | |
|---|---|
| 10.1-13.4 | Galliae, Germania, Britannia, Gallia (Nemausus), Hispaniae (Tarraco), Parthian frontier, Asia, Achaia (Athens), Sicily, Rome |
| 13.4-13.6 | Africa, Rome |
| 13.6-14.5 | Athens, Asia, Cappadocia, Syria, Arabia, Egypt (Pelusium and the Nile) |

There are many difficulties. This listing is by no means complete, and is highly selective, particularly in the final stages, when it appears that the author wearied of his task and narrative. The same thing occurred in the life of Septimius Severus, where that emperor's travels are abruptly brought to an end with the comment, *quoniam longum est minora persequi* (17.5). With no dates and numerous omissions, it is difficult if not hazardous to compile itineraries which will satisfy all, even drawing upon the assistance of coins, inscriptions, and papyri, which furnish several fixed dates upon which a reasonable chronological progression may be anchored. Nonetheless, it is certainly possible that too many provinces have been included in one year, too few in another, and some may indeed warrent shifting. Winters will be spent in the province last mentioned each year, with departure thence no earlier than the following March.

## Appendix IV

121 Gallia
    Germania superior
    Raetia
    Noricum
    Germania superior

122 Germania inferior
    Britannia
    Gallia
    Gallia Narbonensis (Nemausus)
    Hispania (Tarraco)

123 Mauretania (?)
    Africa (?)
    Libya
    Cyrene
    Crete
    Syria
    The Euphrates (Melitene)
    Pontus
    Bithynia
    Asia

124 Thrace
    Moesia
    Dacia
    Pannonia
    Achaia
    Athens

125 Achaia
    Sicily
    Rome

128 Africa
    Rome
    Athens

129 Asia
    Pamphylia
    Phrygia
    Pisidia
    Cilicia

Appendix IV 149

|     | Syria |
|     | Commagene (Samosata) |
|     | Cappadocia |
|     | Pontus |
|     | Syria (Antioch) |

130  Judaea
     Arabia
     Egypt (Nile trip; Alexandria)

131  Libyan desert
     Syria
     Asia
     Athens

132  Rome

134  Syria
     Judaea
     Egypt (?)
     Syria (Antioch)

135  Syria

136  Rome

These itineraries have been conflated in the first instance from those offered by:

    J. Dürr, *Die Reisen des Kaisers Hadrian* (Vienna 1881)

    W. Weber, *Untersuchungen zur Geschichte des Kaisers Hadrianus* (Leipzig 1907)

    B. W. Henderson, *The Life and Principate of the Emperor Hadrian A. D. 76-138* (New York 1923)

    P. L. Strack, *Untersuchungen zur römischen Reichsprägung des zweiten Jahrhunderts. II Die Reichsprägung zur Zeit des Hadrian* (Stuttgart 1933)

APPENDIX V

Second and Third Consulates, Augustus through Hadrian
(in chronological order of the second consulate;
those who reached a third in capital letters)

M. AGRIPPA, I ord. 37, II ord. 28, III ord. 27
T. Statilius Taurus, I suff. 37, II ord. 26

Q. Sanquinius Maximus, I suff. 21 or 22, II suff. 39
L. VITELLIUS, I ord. 34, II ord. 43, III ord. 47
C. Sallustius Passienus Crispus, I suff. 27, II ord. 44
M. Vinicius, I ord. 30, II ord. 45
D. Valerius Asiaticus, I suff. 35, II ord. 46
C. Antistius Vetus, I suff. 46, II ord. 50
C. Suetonius Paulinus, I suff. c. 41, II ord. 66
L. Salvius Otho Titianus, I ord. 52, II suff. 69
L. VERGINIUS RUFUS, I ord. 63, II suff. 69, III ord. 97
C. LICINIUS MUCIANUS, I suff. c. 64, II suff. 70, III suff. 72
T. Flavius Sabinus, I suff. 69, II suff. 72
Ti. Plautius Silvanus Aelianus, I suff. 45, II suff. 74
T. Clodius Eprius Marcellus, I suff. 62, II suff. 74
Q. Petillius Cerialis Caesius Rufus, I suff. 70, II suff. 74[1]
M. Pompeius Silvanus, I suff. 45, II suff. 75?
L. Tampius Flavianus, I suff. anno inc., II suff. 75?
Q. VIBIUS CRISPUS, I suff. c. 62, II suff. 77?, III suff. 83?
A. DIDIUS GALLUS FABRICIUS VEIENTO, I suff. anno inc., II suff. 80, III suff. 83?
Q. Petillius Rufus, I suff. 73?, II ord. 83[1]
T. Aurelius Fulvus, I suff. 70?, II ord. 85
L. Valerius Catullus Messalinus, I suff. 73, II ord. 85
Q. Iulius Cordinus C. Rutilius Gallicus, I suff. 70 or 71, II. suff. 85?
M. Arrecinus Clemens, I suff. 73, II suff. 85
M. Cocceius Nerva, I ord. 71, II ord. 90
A. Lappius Maximus, I suff. 86, II suff. 95
Arrius Antoninus, I suff. 69, II suff. 97?
SEX. IULIUS FRONTINUS, I suff. 73?, II suff. 98, III ord. 100
T. Vestricius Spurinna, I suff. c. 73, II suff. 98
Cn. Domitius Tullus, I suff. c. 79, II suff. 98?
L. IULIUS URSUS, I suff. 84, II suff. 98, III suff. 100
L. IULIUS URSUS SERVIANUS, I suff. 90, II ord. 102, III ord. 134
L. LICINIUS SURA, I suff. c. 97, II ord. 102, III ord. 107

151

Appendix V

M.' Laberius Maximus, I suff. 89, II ord. 103
P. Metilius Sabinus? Nepos, I suff. 91, II suff. 103?
Q. Glitius Atilius Agricola, I suff. 97, II suff. 103
Sex. Attius Suburanus Aemilianus, I suff. 101, II ord. 104
Ti. Iulius Candidus Marius Celsus, I suff. 86, II ord. 105
C. Antius A. Iulius Quadratus, I suff. 94, II ord. 105
Q. Sosius Senecio, I ord. 99, II ord. 107
A. Cornelius Palma Frontonianus, I ord. 99, II ord. 109
L. Publilius Celsus, I suff. 102, II ord. 113
L. Catilius Severus Iulianus Claudius Reginus, I suff. 110, II ord. 120
M. ANNIUS VERUS, I suff. 97, II ord. 121, III ord. 126
M. Lollius Paullinus D. Valerius Asiaticus Saturninus, I suff. 94, II ord. 125
L. Nonius Calpurnius Asprenas Torquatus, I ord. 94, II ord. 128
L. Neratius Marcellus, I suff. 95, II ord. 129
P. Iuventius Celsus T. Aufidius Hoenius Severianus, I suff. c. 115, II ord. 129

This list is based upon Degrassi, *Fasti Consolari*, with amendments and additions suggested by Syme, as recorded in *Tacitus*, Appendix XII, and as incorporated in the volumes of select documents of the imperial reigns edited by McCrum-Woodhead and Smallwood.

1. A. R. Birley, *Britannia* 4 (1973) 179-90, suggests that Q. Petillius Cerialis may have been *cos. III ord.* in 83; that would remove Q. Petillius Rufus' second consulate in that year and thus eliminate him from this list.

APPENDIX VI

Prosopographical Index

From $PIR^2$

P. Acilius Attianus   A 45
Aelius Hadrianus (patruus magnus)   A 183
Aelius Maryllinus (Marullinus)   A 219
Aelius Verus Caesar - see Ceionius (1)
P. Aelius Hadrianus = Imp. Caesar Traianus Hadianus Aug.   A 184
P. Aelius Hadrianus Afer (pater)   A 185
Aemilius - see Messius
Annius Verus - see Ceionius (2)
P. Annius Florus   A 650
Appius Annius Trebonius Gallus   A 692
M. Annius Verus = Imp. Caesar M. Aurelius Antoninus Aug.   A 697
Antinous   A 737
Apollodorus   A 922
Apollonius Syrus   A 928
Q. Articuleius Paetus   A 1177
T. Atilius Rufus Titianus   A 1305
Sex. Attius Suburanus   A 1366; Thomasson, pp. 16-17
T. Aurelius Fulvus Boionius Arrius Antoninus = Imp. Caesar
    T. Aelius Hadrianus Antoninus Aug. Pius   A 1513
C. Avidius Heliodorus   A 1405 (see also H 51)
C. Avidius Nigrinus   A 1408

Q. Baebius Macer   B 20


C. Calpurnius Crassus Frugi Licinianus   C 259
Candidus - See Iulius
L. Catilius Severus Iulianus Claudius Reginus   C 558
L. Ceionius Commodus (1) = L. Aelius Caesar   C 605
L. Ceionius Commodus (2) = L. Aelius Aurelius Commodus = Imp.
    Caesar L. Aurelius Verus Augustus   C 606
Celsus - see Publilius
Ti. Iulius Aquilinus Castricius Saturninus Claudius Livianus
    C 913
A. Cornelius Palma Frontonianus   C 1412
Crassus Frugi - see Calpurnius

Decrianus D 31
Domitia Paulina   D 185

Epictetus  E 74
Eudaemon - see Valerius

Farasmanes - see Pharasmanes
Favorinus  F 123
Florus - see Annius
Fuscus - see Pedanius

Gallus - see Annius

Heliodorus - see Avidius

Ti. Iulius Aquila Polemaeanus  I 168
Ti. Iulius Candidus Marius Celsus  I 241
L. Iulius Ursus Servianus  I 631
P. Iuventius Celsus T. Aufidius Hoenius Severianus  I 882

M.' Laberius Maximus  L 9
L. Licinius Sura  L 253
Livianus - see Claudius
Lusius Quietus  L 439

From PIR

Marcellus - see Neratius and Publicius
Q. Marcius Turbo Fronto Publicius Severus M 179; Thomasson,
    pp. 41-42
L. Marius Maximus Perpetuus Aurelianus  M 233
Maryllinus - see Aelius
Matidia  M 277
M. Cutius Priscus Messius Rusticus Aemilius Papus Arrius Proculus
    Iulius Celsus  M 375

Nepos - see Platorius
L. Neratius Marcellus  N 43
L. Neratius Priscus  N 46
Nigrinus  N 77 = Avidius  A 1408

Palma - see Cornelius
Papus - see Messius
Parthamasiris  P 97 (should be Parthamaspates  P 98)
Paulina - see Domitia
Pedanius Fuscus  P 142

Pharasmanes   P 250
(P. Aelius) Phlegon   P 291
A. Platorius Nepos Aponius Italicus Manilianus C. Licinius
    Pollio   P 337
Plotina - see Pompeia
Polyaenus   P 404 - see Ti. Iulius Aquila Polemaeanus   I 168
Pompeia Plotina   P 509

C. Quinctius Certus Publicius Marcellus   P 779; Thomasson,
    pp. 65-66
L. Publilius Celsus   P 782

Sabina - see Vibia
Salvius Julianus   S 102; Thomasson, pp. 51-52
C. Septicius Clarus   S 302
Servianus - see Iulius
Similis - see Sulpicius
Sosius Papus   S 559 - see M. Cutius Priscus Messius Rusticus
    Aemilius Papus Arrius Proculus Iulius Celsus   M 375
Q. Sosius Senecio   S 560
Suburanus - see Attius
C. Suetonius Tranquillus   S 695
Ser. Sulpicius Similis   S 735
Sura - see Licinius

D. Terentius Gentianus   T 56
Titianus T 186a - see T. Atilius Rufus Titianus   A 1305
Turbo - see Marcius

Valerius Eudaemon absent from PIR; RE Valerius 149
Vibia Sabina Augusta   V 414
C. Ummidius Quadratus   V 603

Additional references are to B.E. Thomasson, *Senatores Procuratoresque Romani* (Göteborg 1975)

BIBLIOGRAPHY

Adams, J.N., "On the authorship of the Historia Augusta," *CQ* 22 (1972) 186-94

Adams, J.N., "The Linguistic Unity of the *Historia Augusta*," *Antichthon* 11 (1977) 93-102

Alexander, P.J., "Letters and Speeches of the Emperor Hadrian," *HSCP* 49 (1938) 141-77

Alföldi, A., *Die monarchische Repräsentation im römischen Kaiserreiche* (Darmstadt 1970)

Alföldy, G., *Die Legionslegaten der römischen Rheinarmeen* (Bonn 1967)

Alföldy, G., "Consuls and Consulars under the Antonines: Prosopography and History," *AncSoc* 7 (1976) 263-99

Aurigemma, S., *Villa Adriana* (Rome 1961)

Aymard, J., *Essai sur les chasses romaines des origines à la fin du siècle des Antonins (Cynegetica)* (Paris 1951)

Baldwin, B., (1) "Hadrian's farewell to life. Some arguments for authenticity," *CQ* 20 (1970) 372-74

Baldwin, B., (2) "Suetonius: Birth, Disgrace, and Death," *AClass* 18 (1975) 61-70

Bardon, H., *Les Empereurs et les Lettres Latines d'Auguste à Hadrien* (Paris 1940)

Barnard, L. W., "Hadrian and Judaism," *JRH* 5 (1969) 285-98

Barnes, T.D., (1) "Hadrian and Lucius Verus," *JRS* 57 (1967) 65-79

Barnes, T.D., (2) "Hadrian's farewell to life," *CQ* 18 (1968) 384-85

Barnes, T.D., (3) *The Sources of the Historia Augusta* (Brussels 1978)

Bauman, R.A., *Impietas in Principem* (Munich 1974)

Beaujeu, J., *La Religion Romaine à l'apogée de l'Empire* I (Paris 1955)

Bengtson, H., *Römische Geschichte* I (Munich 1967)

Benjamin, A.S., "The Altars of Hadrian in Athens and Hadrian's Panhellenic Program," *Hesperia* 32 (1963) 57-86

Béranger, J., (1) "La notion du principat sous Trajan et Hadrien," *Les Empereurs Romains d'Espagne* (Paris 1965) 27-40

Béranger, J., (2) "L'Histoire Auguste. Introduction générale. Aspect politique," *REL* 51 (1973) 26

Béranger, J., (3) "L'hérédité dynastique dans l'Histoire Auguste: Procédé et tradition," *HAC Bonn 1971* (1974) 1-20

Béranger, J., (4) "L'expression du pouvoir suprême dans l'histoire Auguste," *HAC Bonn 1971* (1974) 21-49

Béranger, J., (5) "L'idéologie impériale dans l'Histoire Auguste," *HAC Bonn 1972/1974* (1976) 29-53

Berchem, D. van, *Les Distributions de Blé et d'Argent à la Plèbe Romaine sous l'Empire* (Geneva 1939)

Bertinelli Angeli, M.G., "I 'Dodici Cesari' nell'Historia Augusta (confronto con Tacito e Suetonio)," *Studi L. DeRegibus* (Genoa 1969) 145-66

Bickerman, E., "Diva Augusta Marciana," *AJP* 95 (1974) 362-76

Birley, A.R., (1) "The Oath not to put Senators to death," *CR* 12 (1962) 197-99

Birley, A.R., (2) "The Augustan History," in T.A. Dorey, *Latin Biography* (London 1967) 113-38

Birley, A.R., (3) "Petillius Cerialis and the Conquest of Brigantia," *Britannia* 4 (1973) 179-90

Birley, A.R., (4) *Lives of the Later Caesars* (Harmondsworth 1976)

Birley, E., (1) "Senators in the Emperors' Service," *PBA* 39 (1953) 197-214

Birley, E., (2) "Hadrianic Frontier Policy," *Carnuntina* (Graz-Cologne 1956) 25-33

Birley, E., (3) "Africana in the Historia Augusta," *HAC Bonn 1968/69* (1970) 79-90

Bonner, S.F., *Education in Ancient Rome* (Berkeley/Los Angeles 1977)

Borzsák, S., "Zum Hadriansgedicht Animula vagula blandula," *ACD* 4 (1968) 101-05

Bourne, F.C., "The Roman Alimentary Program and Italian Agriculture," *TAPA* 91 (1960) 47-75

Bowersock, G.W., (1) *Greek Sophists in the Roman Empire* (Oxford 1969)

Bowersock, G.W., (2) "Suetonius and Trajan," *Hommages M. Renard* (Brussels 1969) 119-25

Bowie, E.L., "Greeks and their Past in the Second Sophistic," *P&P* 46 (1970) 3-41

Brown, F.E., "Hadrianic Architecture," *Essays in Honor of Karl Lehmann* (New York 1964) 55-58

Brunt, P.A., "Charges of Provincial Maladministration under the Early Principate," *Historia* 10 (1961) 189-227

Bühler, W., "Ein unbekanntes, Kaiser Hadrian zugeschriebenes Epigramm," *ZPE* 31 (1978) 55-60

Bulle, H., "Ein Jagddenkmal des Kaisers Hadrian," *JDAI* 34 (1919) 144-72

Burian, J., "Der Gegensatz zwischen Rom und den Barbaren in der *Historia Augusta*," *Eirene* 15 (1977) 55-96

Burian, J., "*Fides historica* als methodologischer Grundsatz der *Historia Augusta*," *Klio* 59 (1977) 285-98

Buschor, E., "Die hadrianischen Jagdbilder," *RM* 38-39 (1923-24) 52-54

Cameron, A., "Paganism and Literature in Late Fourth Century Rome," *Christianisme et Formes Littéraires* (Geneva 1977) 1-30

Cantarelli, L., "Gli scritti latini di Adriano imp.," *Studi e docum. di storia e diritto* 19 (1898) 113-70

Carandini, A., *Vibia Sabina* (Florence 1969)

Carney, T.F., "The Political Legends on Hadrian's Coinage. Policies and Problems," *Turtle* 6 (1967) 291-303

Carney, T.F., "How Suetonius' lives reflect on Hadrian," *PACA* 11 (1968) 7-24

Cazzaniga, I., "Il tetrapharmacum cibo adrianeo (H.A. Spart., Vit. Hadr. 21,4, Vit. Ael. 5,4 e Philod. P. Herc. 1005, IV, 10). Esegesi e critica testuale," *Poesia latina in frammenti* (Genoa 1974) 359-66

Centerwell, I., *Spartiani Vita Hadriani commentario illustrata. Disputatio prior.* (Upsala 1870)

Champlin, E., "Hadrian's Heir," *ZPE* 21 (1976) 78-89

Chastognol, A., "L'Histoire Auguste et les 'Douze Césars' de Suétone," *HAC Bonn 1970* (1972) 109-23

Chowen, R.H., (1) "Traveling Companions of Hadrian," *CJ* 50 (1954-55) 122-24

Chowen, R.H., (2) "Nature of Hadrian's Theatron at Daphne," *AJA* 60 (1956) 275-77

Chowen, R., (3) "The problem of Hadrian's visits to North Africa," *CJ* 65 (1969-70) 323-24

Clairmont, Chr.W., *Die Bildnisse des Antinous* (Rome 1966)

Clarke, M.L., *Higher Education in the Ancient World* (London 1971)

Clemente, G., "Storia amministrativa e falsificazione nella *Historia Augusta*," *RFIC* 100 (1972) 108-23

Cramer, F.H., *Astrology in Roman Law and Politics* (Philadelphia 1954)

Crook, J., (1) *Consilium Principis* (Cambridge 1955)

Crook, J., (2) "*Suetonius ab epistulis*," *PCPS* 4 (1956-57) 18-22

Daly, L.W., and W. Suchier, *Altercatio Hadriani Augusti et Epicteti Philosophi* (Urbana, Ill., 1939)

Damsholt, T., "Zur Benutzung von dem *Breviarium* des Eutrop in der *Historia Augusta*," *C&M* 25 (1964) 138-50

Davies, R.W., (1) "Fronto, Hadrian and the Roman army," *Latomus* 27 (1968) 75-95

Davies, R.W., (2) "The Roman Military Diet," *Britannia* 2 (1971) 122-42

Day, J., *An Economic History of Athens under Roman Domination* (New York 1942)

Dehner, S., *Hadriani reliquiae* I (Bonn 1883)

de Kisch, Y., (1) "Les sortes vergilianae dans l'Histoire Auguste," *MEFR* 82 (1970) 321-62

de Kisch, Y., (2) "Sur quelques *omina imperii* dans *l'Histoire Auguste*," *REL* 51 (1973) 190-207

den Boer, W., (1) "Religion and Literature in Hadrian's Policy," *Mnemosyne* 8 (1955) 123-44

den Boer, W., (2) "Trajan's Deification and Hadrian's Succession," *AncSoc* 6 (1975) 203-12

Dilke, O.A.W., "The Literary Output of the Roman Emperors," *G&R* 4 (1957) 78-97

Dobias, J., "A propos de *l'expeditio Suebica et Sarmatica* de l'empereur Hadrien en l'an 118," *Omagiu Daicoviciu* (Bucharest 1960) 147-53

d'Ors, A., "La Signification de l'oeuvre d'Hadrien dans l'histoire du droit romain," *Les Empereurs Romains d'Espagne* (Paris 1965) 147-58

Dürr, J., *Die Reisen des Kaisers Hadrians* (Vienna 1881)

Duncan-Jones, R., "The Purpose and Organisation of the Alimenta," *PBSR* 32 (1964) 123-46

Eck, W., *Senatoren von Vespasian bis Hadrian* (Munich 1970)

Fink, R.O., "Hunt's *Pridianum*: British Museum Papyrus 2851," *JRS* 48 (1958) 102-16

Fitzgibbon, J.C., "Ergastula," *Class. News and Views* 20 (1976) 55-58

Follet, S.,(1) "Hadrien en Égypte et en Judée," *RPh* 42 (1968) 54-77

Follet, S.,(2) *Athènes au $II^e$ et au $III^e$ Siècle* (Paris 1976)

Frere, S.S., *Britannia* (London 1974[2])

Freudenberger, R., *Das Verhalten der römischen Behörden gegen die Christen im 2. Jahrhundert* (Munich 1967)

Frezza, P., "L'organizzazione municipale fra Traiano e Adriano," *Labeo* 20 (1974) 234-41

Fuks, A., "The Jewish Revolt in Egypt (A.D. 115-117) in the light of the papyri," *Aegyptus* 33 (1953) 131-58

Gagé, J., *Basiléia. Les Césars, Les Rois d'Orient et Les Mages* (Paris 1968)

Gallavotti, C., "Animula nudula," *Maia* 23 (1971) 297-302

Garnsey, P., "Trajan's alimenta. Some Problems," *Historia* 17 (1968) 367-81

Gascou, J., "Nouvelles données chronologiques sur la carrière de Suétone," *Latomus* 37 (1978) 436-44

Gilliam, J.F., (1) "An Egyptian Cohort in A.D. 117," *HAC Bonn 1964/65* (1966) 91-97

Gilliam, J.F., (2) "Ammianus and the Historia Augusta: The Lost Books and the Period 117-285," *HAC Bonn 1970* (1972) 125-47

Graindor, P., *Athènes sous Hadrien* (Cairo 1934)

Gray, W.D., "A Political Ideal of the Emperor Hadrian," *Ann. Report of the AHA* (1914) I 115-24

Gray, W.D., *A Study of the Life of Hadrian Prior to his Accession* (Smith College Studies in History 1919)

Gray, W.D. "The Founding of Aelia Capitolina and the Chronology of the Jewish War Under Hadrian," *AJSL* 39 (1922-23) 248-56

Gray, W.D. "New Light from Egypt on the Early Reign of Hadrian," *AJSL* 40 (1923-24) 14-29

Guarducci, M., "La religione di Adriano," *Les Empereurs Romains d'Espagne* (Paris 1965) 209-19

Gullini, G., "Apollodoro e Adriano. Ellenismo e classicismo nell'architettura romana," *BA* 53 (1968 [1971]) 63-80

Hänel, G., *Corpus legum ab imperatoribus Romanis ante Justinianum latarum* (Leipzig 1857)

Hammond, M., (1) "A Statue of Trajan represented on the *Anaglypha Traiani*," *MAAR* 21 (1953) 127-83

Hammond, M., (2) "Composition of the Senate, A.D. 68-235," *JRS* 47 (1957) 74-81

Hammond, M., (3) *The Antonine Monarchy* (Rome 1959)

Hands, A.R., *Charities and Social Aid in Greece and Rome* (Ithaca, N.Y., 1968)

Harris, R., "Hadrian's decree of expulsion of the Jews from Jerusalem," *HTR* 19 (1926) 199-206

Henderson, B.W., *The Life and Principate of the Emperor Hadrian A.D. 76-138* (New York 1923)

Herrmann, L., "La réplique d'Hadrien à Florus," *Latomus* 9 (1950) 385-87

Hicks, R., "The Religious Policy of the Emperor Hadrian," *TPAPA* 70 (1939) 36

Hohl, E., "Über das Problem der Historia Augusta," *WS* 71 (1958) 132-52

Hohl, E., *Historia Augusta* I (Zürich/Munich 1976)

Isaac, B., and I. Roll, "Judaea in the Early Years of Hadrian's Reign," *Latomus* 38 (1979) 54-66

Johne, K.-P., "Zur stadtrömischen Tendenz der Historia Augusta," *WZRostock* 18 (1969) 463-67

Johne, K.-P., "Zur Bedeutung der Stadtpräfektur in der Historia Augusta," *Actes de la XII$^e$ conférence 'Eirene'* (Bucharest/Amsterdam 1975) 403-09

Johne, K.-P., *Kaiserbiographie und Senatsaristokratie. Untersuchungen zur Datierung und sozialen Herkunft der Historia Augusta* (Berlin 1976)

Johne, K.-P., "Die *Epitome de Caesaribus* und die *Historia Augusta*," *Klio* 59 (1977) 497-501

Jones, C.P., "Sura and Senecio," *JRS* 60 (1970) 98-104

Jones, T.B., *The Silver-Plated Age* (Sandoval, N.M., 1962)

Kähler, H., *Hadrian und seine Villa bei Tivoli* (Berlin 1950)

Kaser, M., *Das römische Privatrecht* (Munich 1971$^2$)

Kennedy, G., *The Art of Rhetoric in the Roman World* (Princeton 1972)

Keppie, L.J.F., "The legionary garrison of Judaea under Hadrian," *Latomus* 32 (1973) 859-64

Kerler, G., *Die Aussenpolitik in der Historia Augusta* (Bonn 1971)

Kienast, D., "Hadrian, Augustus und die eleusinischen Mysterien," *JNG* 10 (1959-60) 61-69

Koeppel, G., "Profectio und Adventus," *BJ* 169 (1969) 130-94

Kolb, F., "Die Paenula in der Historia Augusta," *HAC Bonn 1971* (1974) 81-101

Lécrivain, Ch., *Études sur l'histoire Auguste* (Paris 1904)

Leo, F., *Die Griechisch-Römische Biographie* (Leipzig 1901)

Levi, A.C., "Hadrian as King of Egypt," *NC* (1948) 30-40

Liebmann-Frankfort, Th., "Les Juifs dans l'*Histoire Auguste*," *Latomus* 33 (1974) 579-607

Loane, H.A., "The Sortes Vergilianae," *CW* 21 (1927-28) 185-89

Lugli, G., *Roma Antica - Il Centro Monumentale* (Rome 1946)

MacDonald, W.L., *The Pantheon* (Cambridge, Mass., 1976)

MacMullen, R., "Roman Imperial Building in the Provinces," *HSCP* 64 (1959) 207-35

Magie, D., *The Scriptores Historiae Augustae*, three vols. (London & Cambridge, Mass., 1921-32)

Mariotti, I., "Animula vagula blandula," *Studia A. Ronconi* (Rome 1970) 233-49

Marrou, H.I., *A History of Education in Antiquity* (London 1956)

Martin, J.P., "Hadrien et le Phénix. Propagande numismatique," *Mélanges William Seston* (Paris 1974) 327-37

Mattingly, H., (1) "Some Historical Coins of Hadrian," *JRS* 15 (1925) 209-22

Mattingly, H., (2) "The Religious Background of the 'Historia Augusta,'" *HTR* 39 (1946) 213-15

Mattingly, H., (3) "Some very odd Latin," *G&R* 16 (1947) 88-89

Maull, I., "Hadrians Jagddenkmal," *JOEAI* 42 (1955) 53-67

Mayer, R., "Two Notes on Latin Poets," *PCPS* 202 (1976) 57-59

Mazzarino, S., "Precetti del buon governo (Praecepta gubernandae rei p.) e problemi di economia militare," *HAC Bonn 1971* (1974) 103-12

McDermott, W.C., (1) "SHA Vita Hadriani II, 1-6," *Mnemosyne* 22 (1969) 186-90

McDermott, W.C., (2) "Stemmata quid faciunt? The Descendants of Frontinus," *AncSoc* 7 (1976) 229-61

Merten, E., "Die Adoption Hadrians," *Bonner Festgabe J. Straub* (Bonn 1977) 247-59

Metcalf, W.E., "Hadrian, Iovis Olympius," *Mnemosyne* 27 (1974) 59-66

Millar, F., *The Emperor in the Roman World* (Ithaca, N.Y., 1977)

Mouchová, B., (1) "Omina mortis in der Historia Augusta," *HAC Bonn 1968/1969* (1970) 111-49

Mouchová, B., (2) *Untersuchungen über die Scriptores Historiae Augustae* (Prague 1975)

Mylonas, G., *Eleusis and the Eleusinian Mysteries* (Princeton 1961)

Nash, E., *Pictorial Dictionary of Ancient Rome* (London 1961-62)

Nierhaus, R., "Hadrians Verhältnis zu Italica," *Corolla E. Swoboda* (Graz 1966) 151-68

Oliver, J.H., (1) "Documents Concerning the Emperor Hadrian," *Hesperia* 10 (1941) 361-70

Oliver, J.H., (2) "The Divi of the Hadrianic Period," *HTR* 42 (1949) 35-40

Oliver, J.H., (3) "Hadrian's precedent, the alleged initiation of Philip II," *AJP* 71 (1950) 295-99

Oliver, J.H., (4) "The Athens of Hadrian," *Les Empereurs Romains d'Espagne* (Paris 1965) 123-32

Oliver, J.H., (5) "The Ancestry of Gordian I," *AJP* 89 (1968) 345-47

Oliver, J.H., (6) "Hadrian's epistle to the Dionysiac artists at Athens," *AAA* 7 (1974) 118-19

Pekáry, T., "Das Grab des Pompeius," *HAC Bonn 1970* (1972) 195-98

Pepe, L., "Questioni Adrianee. Appio Annio Trebonio Gallo (*hist. Aug. Hadr.* 2,7)," *GIF* 14 (1961) 69-75

Perowne, S. *Hadrian* (London 1960)

Perry, B.E., *Secundus the Silent Philosopher* (Chapel Hill, N.C., 1964)

Peter, H., *Die Scriptores Historiae Augustae* (Leipzig 1892)

Peter, H., *Historicorum Romanorum Reliquiae* II (Leipzig 1906)

Pflaum, H.-G., (1) *Les Carrières Procuratoriennes Équestres sous le Haut-Empire Romain* I-IV (Paris 1960-61)

Pflaum, H.-G., (2) "Le règlement successoral d'Hadrien," *HAC Bonn 1963* (1964) 95-122

Pflaum, H.-G., (3) "Tendances politiques et administratives au II siècle de notre ère," *REL* 42 (1964) 112-21

Pflaum, H.-G., (4) "Un ami inconnu d'Hadrien: M. Aemilius Papus," *Klio* 46 (1965) 331-37

Pflaum, H.-G., (5) "La Valeur de la Source Inspiratrice de la Vita Hadriani et de la Vita Marci Antonini à la lumière des personnalités contemporaines nommément citées," *HAC Bonn 1968/1969* (1970) 173-99

Picard, Ch., "Chronique de la Sculpture Étrusco-Latine (1940-1950) II. Principat d'Hadrien," *REL* 30 (1952) 347-73

Pringsheim, F., "The Legal Policy and Reforms of Hadrian," *JRS* 24 (1934) 141-53

Raubitschek, A.E., "Hadrian as the Son of Zeus Eleutherios," *AJA* 49 (1945) 128-33

Ronconi, A., "Interpolazioni al testo della 'Hist. Aug.'?" *SIFC* 9 (1931) 25-35

Roos, A.G., "Ad Spartiani vitam Hadriani," *Mnemosyne* 41 (1913) 144

Scarborough, J., *Roman Medicine* (Ithaca, N.Y., 1969)

Schanz, M., and C. Hosius, *Geschichte der römischen Literatur* III (Munich 1922$^3$)

Schiller, A.A., "Sententiae Hadriani de re militari," *Sein und Werden im Recht. Festgabe für U. von Lübtow* (Berlin 1970) 295-306

Schiller, A.A., "'Alimenta' in the 'Sententiae Hadriani'," *Studi G. Grosso* IV (Turin 1971) 399-415

Schiller, A.A., "Vindication of a Repudiated Text 'Sententiae et Epistolae Hadriani', *La Critica del Testo* (Florence 1971) 717-27

Schulz, O.T., *Leben des Kaisers Hadrian* (Leipzig 1904)

Schwartz, J., (1) refutation of S. Follet, *CE* 44 (1969) 164-68

Schwartz, J., (2) "Éléments suspects de la Vita Hadriani," *HAC Bonn 1972/1974* (1976) 239-67

Seyfarth, W., "Vom Geschichtsschreiber und seinem Publikum im spätantiken Rom," *WZRostock* 18 (1969) 449-55

Sijpesteijn, P.D., "A New Document Concerning Hadrian's Visit to Egypt," *Historia* 18 (1969) 109-18

Sinnigen, W.G., "The Origins of the *Frumentarii*," *MAAR* 27 (1962) 213-24

Smallwood, E.M., (1) *Documents Illustrating the Principates of Nerva, Trajan and Hadrian* (Cambridge 1966)

Smallwood, E.M., (2) *The Jews Under Roman Rule* (Leiden 1976)

Stein, A., *Römische Inschriften in der antiken Literatur* (Prague 1931)

Stertz, S., "Christianity in the *Historia Augusta*," *Latomus* 36 (1977) 694-715

Stinespring, W.F., "Hadrian in Palestine 129/130 A.D.," *JAOS* 59 (1939) 360-65

Strack, P.L., *Untersuchungen zur römischen Reichsprägung des zweiten Jahrhunderts. II Die Reichspragung des Hadrian* (Stuttgart 1933)

Straub, J., *Regeneratio imperii* (Darmstadt 1972)

Straub, J., "Juristische Notizen in der Historia Augusta," *Actes de la XII$^e$ conférence 'Eirene'* (Bucharest/Amsterdam 1975) 383-401

Stroheker, K.F., "Die Aussenpolitik des Antoninus Pius nach der Historia Augusta," *HAC Bonn 1964/1965* (1966) 241-56

Suerbaum, W., *Vom antiken zum frühmittelalterlichen Staatsbegriff* (Münster 1970$^2$)

Syme, R., (1) "The jurist Neratius Priscus," *Hermes* 85 (1957) 480-93

Syme, R., (2) *Tacitus* (Oxford 1958)

Syme, R., (3) "Piso Frugi and Crassus Frugi," *JRS* 50 (1960) 12-20

Syme, R., (4) "The Wrong Marcius Turbo," *JRS* 52 (1962) 87-96

Syme, R., (5) "Hadrian and Italica," *JRS* 54 (1964) 142-49

Syme, R., (6) "Hadrian the Intellectual," *Les Empereurs Romains d'Espagne* (Paris 1965) 243-49

Syme, R., (7) *Ammianus and the Historia Augusta* (Oxford 1968)

Syme, R., (8) "Fiction and Archaeology in the Fourth Century," *Tardo Antico e Alto Medioevo. La Forma Artistica nel Passaggio dall'Antichità al Medioevo* (Accad. Naz. dei Lincei, anno 365, Quaderno 105, Rome 1968) 23-30

Syme, R., (9) "Hadrian in Moesia," *Arheoloski Vestnik* 19 (1968) 101-09 = *Danubian Papers* (Bucharest 1971) 204-12

Syme, R., (10) "The Ummidii," *Historia* 17 (1968) 72-105

Syme, R., (11) *Emperors and Biography* (Oxford 1971)

Syme, R., (12) *The Historia Augusta. A Call of Clarity* (Bonn 1971)

Syme, R., (13) "The Composition of the Historia Augusta: Recent Theories," *JRS* 62 (1972) 123-33

Syme, R., (14) "Astrology in the Historia Augusta," *HAC Bonn 1972/1974* (1976) 291-309

Syme, R., (15) "Propaganda in the Historia Augusta," *Latomus* 37 (1978) 173-92

Szelest, H., "Zur Kompositionsart der Historia Augusta (Exkurse u. ihre Rolle in der Sammlung)," *WZRostock* 18 (1969) 457-62

Szelest, H., "Les digressions chez les auteurs de l'Histoire Auguste," *Eos* 58 (1969-70) 115-23

Szelest, H., "Rolle und Aufgaben der Reden und Briefe in der 'Historia Augusta'," *Eos* 59 (1971) 325-38

Tandoi, V., "Restauri testuali nell'Historia Augusta," *SIFC* 43 (1971) 101-14

Taylor, L.R., and T.R.S. Broughton, "The Order of the Consuls' Names in the Yearly Lists," *MAAR* 19 (1949) 1-14

Thornton, M.K., "Hadrian and his Reign," *ANRW* II 2 (Berlin/New York 1975) 432-76

Townend, G.B., "Suetonius and his Influence," in T.A. Dorey, *Latin Biography* (London 1967) 79-111

Travlos, J., *Pictorial Dictionary of Ancient Athens* (New York 1971)

Trowbridge, M.L., "Folklore in the SHA," *CP* 33 (1938) 69-88

van Groningen, B.A., "Preparatives to Hadrian's Visit to Egypt," *Studi A. Calderini* II (Milan 1956) 253-56

Walton, F.R., "Religious Thought in the Age of Hadrian," *Numen* 4 (1957) 165-70

Watson, G.R., *The Roman Soldier* (Ithaca, N.Y., 1969)

Weber, W., *Untersuchungen zur Geschichte des Kaisers Hadrianus* (Leipzig 1907)

Webster, G., *The Roman Imperial Army* (London 1969)

White, P., "The authorship of the Historia Augusta," *JRS* 57 (1967) 115-33

Williams, W., "Hadrian and the Antonine emperors as patrons of Greek cities," *PCA* 77 (1975) 24-25

Wilson, L.M., *The Clothing of the Ancient Romans* (Baltimore 1938)

Wissowa, G., *Religion und Kultus der Römer* (Munich 1912$^2$)

Ziegler, K.-H., *Die Beziehungen zwischen Rom und dem Partherreich* (Wiesbaden 1964)

Zoepffel, R., "Hadrian und Numa," *Chiron* 8 (1978) 391-427

www.ingramcontent.com/pod-product-compliance
Ingram Content Group UK Ltd.
Pitfield, Milton Keynes, MK11 3LW, UK
UKHW041428180426
11947UKWH00007B/349